After Sylvia

After Sylvia

Poems and Essays in Celebration
of Sylvia Plath

Edited by Sarah Corbett & Ian Humphreys

Nine
Arches
Press

After Sylvia
Poems and Essays in Celebration of Sylvia Plath
Edited by Sarah Corbett & Ian Humphreys

ISBN: 978-1-913437-56-5
eISBN: 978-1-913437-57-2

First published October 2022 by:

Nine Arches Press
Unit 14, Sir Frank Whittle Business Centre,
Great Central Way, Rugby.
CV21 3XH
United Kingdom

www.ninearchespress.com

Printed in the United Kingdom by:
Imprint Digital

Nine Arches Press is supported using public funding by Arts Council England.

Supported using public funding by
**ARTS COUNCIL
ENGLAND**

To our mothers,

Sonia Calhoun

and in memory of
Teresa Humphreys

The clear vowels rise like balloons.
– Sylvia Plath, 'Morning Song'

Contents

Ian Humphreys

A Celebration: Writing *After Sylvia*

After Sylvia pays tribute to one of the most important voices of twentieth-century English language poetry. It also celebrates beginnings. Published during Sylvia Plath's birthday month, this anthology honours the 90th anniversary of her birth on October 27, 1932.

There are sixty pieces of new writing in *After Sylvia*, and the majority are commissions. Each featured poem and essay, in some way, takes inspiration from Plath, her work, her genius, and her vision.

We asked our poets and scholars to write towards one of five Plathian themes: *Rebirth, Womanhood, Magic, Mothers & Fathers,* and *Nature*. These themes are illuminated through five key chapters, each comprised of eleven poems and one essay. Sarah and I gave contributors free rein to interpret the Plathian themes however they wished. The result is a book of beauty, power, depth, and surprises.

Perhaps instinctively, many of the poems and essays touch on more than one of the themes we asked authors to explore. This blurring of boundaries feels true to life, and brings a sense of harmony to the anthology, as does a shared interest in broader Plathian themes, such as illness, childbirth, despair, patriarchy, joy and hope. Many of the poems echo Plath's refusal to look away from uncomfortable truths, and in some pieces, her most admired stylistic traits are held up to the light, including her startling imagery, confessional narratives, and dark humour.

After Sylvia begins with Emily Berry's 'Last Poem', which itself starts with these apposite words:

"We don't forget / we don't forget"

Today, Sylvia Plath is remembered and revered more than ever. Consider the book's final poem by Nina Billard Sarmadi, who was ten years old when her contribution won the Young Poets Network's Sylvia Plath challenge (Plath herself was eight when her first poem was published in the *Boston Herald*). Nina's success underlines the importance of Sylvia Plath to younger readers and authors. In 2018, when the Poetry Society conducted a global survey to discover which poets young people most admired, Plath came out on top, above Shakespeare.

Three international poetry competitions, spearheaded by The Sylvia Plath Prize, helped to shape *After Sylvia*. Between them, they attracted thousands of submissions from all around the world, with over a dozen prize-winning and commended poems selected for publication. By bringing a competition element to the anthology, we hoped to discover some new and exciting voices, and indeed several of the successful entries were written by poets at the outset of their creative journey.

"Love set you going like a fat gold watch" is the opening line of 'Morning Song', and the very first words in Plath's ground-breaking, posthumous collection *Ariel*. In no-small way, love was the catalyst for this book. Plath holds a special place in the hearts and minds of countless readers and writers. Personally, I came to Plath in my teens through her novel, *The Bell Jar*. The book, and later Plath's compelling poetry, revealed to me the potency of language, how a perfectly formed line can jolt your senses, make you look at the world and yourself differently.

Of course, words have the power to injure as well as inspire, and *After Sylvia* is more than just a love letter to Plath. For example, Degna Stone's essay discusses with Plathian candour the problematic language and tropes in some of Plath's work:

> 'I choose to dip in and out of Plath's poetry, avoiding the poems that exclude me … and enjoying the poems that give me hope, make me smile or remind me that poetry can rescue you from despair just in the nick of time.'

Therapeutic. Disturbing. Fearless. Dazzling. Plath's writing means many things to so many people. In *After Sylvia*, Plath's trademark daring and originality have emboldened some contributors to take risks with style, form, voice and subject matter, with each chapter lit by poems that are surprising in scope and ambition.

We hope you enjoy immersing yourself in *After Sylvia*, and are moved by its wealth of thought-provoking new beginnings. Although indebted to a great, inspiring voice from the past, the anthology looks steadfastly to the future, bearing witness to the power and complexity of Sylvia Plath's thriving legacy.

Sarah Corbett

An Exploration: Writing After Sylvia Plath

How do we write after Sylvia Plath? For me, and for many of the poets and scholars writing *After Sylvia* for this anthology, this is a question we will have asked ourselves at some point in our journey towards becoming a poet, a writer, a scholar; often the question doesn't ever entirely go away. Many of the writers represented here have expressed a sense of honour on receiving a commission to write *After Sylvia*, but also the anxiety of responding adequately; how *do we* write back to this mighty poet?

Many of us will have precious 'origin stories' of how we first encountered her work. For some of us it was through an enlightened teacher, for others a surreptitious or even semi-magical encounter – copies of *Ariel* slipping from library shelves, or even stolen, as Tiffany Atkinson recounts in her powerful and haunting poem 'Small flame for Sylvia', "every poet-girl who ever knelt / in Blackwell's on a dreary half-term afternoon." Or sometimes the first encounter was entirely accidental, as happened to Gail Crowther one stormy afternoon in her school library. By chance she opened a volume of Plath and fell irretrievably into the opening lines of 'Mirror', "I am silver and exact." One thing seems to be universal: once encountered, and fallen in love with, Plath's writing never leaves us.

But it can leave us with a problem: it's not *easy* to write after Sylvia. In the poems of *Ariel* – both the 1965 edition that made her famous, and the *Restored Ariel*, the manuscript Plath left on her desk when she died that famously 'begins with love and ends with spring', we encounter an artist so achieved, so arrived and complete, a vision so startling, beautiful, and terrifying, that it can leave us to ask *how do we write after Sylvia*? Let's face it, she pretty much nailed it: *Ariel* is the work of perhaps one of the most important poetic geniuses of the twentieth century. But instead of silencing us, she *helps us* to find our voice, she gives us permission to speak powerfully from our centre, wherever that is; to take risks, take no prisoners, tell the bald truth as we see it, however uncomfortable it might be for us, or for our reader.

To become a poet we must break free of our influences, 'find our voice,' chart our own course into that unmappable territory. Sylvia Plath is one of those influences that we carry with us. I was introduced to two Sylvia Plath poems by an A Level English teacher – 'Mushrooms' and 'Elm' – and without knowing who had written them, experienced a hit of recognition – wordless, in the gut, an acknowledgement of power and, yes, darkness I could not ignore. She was the first female poet I read, and became very quickly the most important writer in my own poetic development. My mentor would write little 'SP' notes in the margins of my poems, pointing out where Plath's influence was too strong, or where I'd ventriloquised whole lines. This intervention was essential – I had to find my own voice – but as I've got older, I've come to look upon these 'SPs' in the margins' as marks of a guiding spirit.

The poets and scholars in this volume of newly commissioned poems and essays have found their voices *after* Sylvia, *through* Sylvia, in many cases *because of* Sylvia. But the work of each poet is distinct in its expression of a unique voice, a unique vision. Many of the poets represented here have been publishing for decades: poets such as Ruth Fainlight, Penelope Shuttle, Caroline Bird and Pascale Petit; others have made their name in more recent years, such as Mona Arshi, Emily Berry, Mary Jean Chan and Romalyn Ante; still others are emerging poets, yet to publish a full collection, such as Daniel Fraser, Julie Irigaray and Jennifer Lee Tsai. The range of essays comes to us from Plath biographer Heather Clark, Plath scholar Gail Crowther, Ledbury Emerging Critic Devina Shah, emerging scholar Dorka Tamás, and poet and critic Degna Stone. Each work responds to, explores, writes in the wake of, the influence of Sylvia Plath, a writer who in her brief life created a legacy for generations of writers to follow.

REBIRTH

Emily Berry

Last Poem

We don't forget   we don't forget
All night your stars   blaze on the hill
Which is to say   all our lives
Childhood shut fast   behind a door
My mother, too   built a room that
she would later   die in. She dug her
own grave in the air   And in the small
backyard there was   a stone lion
a thicket of ivy   And in the house
there were books   But the words
that were there   were not omens
of death, they are alive   And everything
you wrote is alive   So tip the milk
back into the jug   Take the blanket
from the crack   under the door
Come back, come back   from the beyond
where the moon   stays sad all night
but doesn't hurt   it doesn't hurt
when the clock   runs backwards
and, survivor   you are older
than you could ever   have imagined
and there's still time   still time
for you to write   your last poem
in praise of long life.

i.m. Paula Neuss & Sylvia Plath

Jacob Polley

The Expulsion

She was wearing the white of a clock face. She would not sit on a dusty bench, nor risk a pistachio ice cream, nor look at the clock itself, which was set high above her in the façade of the loggia. She had always forsaken archways and shade. The fierceness of her mind was the fierceness of the sunlit empty square. In the red dust, silver wrappers shrivelled. It could have been the morning after a burning alive, when the city had paid someone to sweep up and shovel the ash and bits of burnt bone into the river, but she would not look at the clock.

She could hear the counting of small coins several streets away. She hadn't got the hang of the money. He'd told her over and over again that the big coins were worth less than the small and that the city owed its formal gardens and statuary to Renaissance bankers who lived on hillsides, high above the streets and the counting of small coins. But she was always counting. Anyone could see the numbers in her face, he'd told her. Go and stand in front of a masterpiece, he'd told her.

Behind a great wooden door studded with iron was a sky of lapis lazuli confined to the wall of a cool side chapel. Even as she stood in silence in her white shift, goosebumps on her arms, it occurred to her that someone must have brought the eggs, warm from the coop, for the binding of the pigment, just as someone must have supplied the logs and kindling, and someone else must have been paid to pile up the logs and kindling in the main square. The same thought had occurred to Eve, just outside the garden gate. Anyone could see it in her miserable painted mouth.

We're in the city of history, he'd told her. What mattered was that she be exposed to architecture and statues, gardens and frescoes. She wasn't to think of hencoops and shopping lists. She stood. She was exposed. It was agony, the thought of the woodcutter trundling home with coins in his purse, whistling a tune. After all, it wasn't his bare feet blackening in the fire. He'd been able to turn away as the fatty smoke billowed into the sky.

Tom Weir

Walking with Annie

What is it for, this night –
the compromise
it makes with the city

to call off its threat
the way you might draw
a pack of dogs from the scent.

Just you and me, little fox –
sack of skin and bone
I carry close to my chest

as we head further into the dark
than I've ever been –
so dark the river below

has become an imagined place.
We've been here each night
since the week you were born

but never this late.
Look how vulnerable
you've made the dawn.

Mary Jean Chan

The Painter
Golden Shovel after Sylvia Plath's 'Mushrooms'

Last spring, I thought of nothing but the sullen cities, their silence, but overnight you began painting, took colours I had not heard of and made our four walls very much alive. It was thrilling to learn you all over again: the wash glowing whitely on canvas, the calm movement of your hand. I never knew you'd drawn discreetly as a child. I think my enthusiasm took you by surprise, but I couldn't help it! Very soon the autumn leaves you love will be turning the colour of rust so we'll quietly make our way through an anguished or peaceful hour, holding the year inside our painted scene, imagined and factual like hope, comforting as soil beneath our toes.

Tamar Yoseloff

New Year

Cloud veils houses and cars,
the drowsy street.

Tears hang from bare
branches, small offerings

for the season of fresh starts,
all those resolutions like cut pines
lined up for the bin men;

for poems struck through,
a thought nearly born before words
disintegrate, brittle petals.

The forecast is bitter.
Cracks in the pavement
are wide enough to fall into

and there will be no one
to lift you, just a crow
sounding his old alarm.

Polly Atkin

Not Dying

Not dying is not the same as being
reborn. You may feel like it – shaking like a foal –
after fever. Not dying might feel like life
but life is not not dying. It is merely
going on. There's no miracle in that. Coming to
and realising your heart is intact and not
gone off as you thought in the night – that your arm
has not exploded – your throat not closed –
that you passed through the pit of a hundred centuries
and rose up like the sun, a gold lion pawing
at your sickness, and yes, lying down is not dying
even when you would rather pull up the turf
to your chin like a blanket and sleep a long sleep
in the dark of the earth, starless, because
being upright is not not falling anymore
than falling is the same as failing, anymore
than the moon is sad because her mouth is open,
giving out what she has taken, as though not hoarding
what was never your own is generous. The moon
is no plagiarist. Only she can do what she does.
Nothing is made out of nothing.
We lie down, we get up. Something is lost
or gained. Or both. We are dying quicker
or slower than we think. This is my secret.
I keep passing myself from night to day
so a light is always shining.

Romalyn Ante

Pilgrimage to Mindanao

To clear the air means to remove bad feelings
between two hearts. This tree and I – our
exhalations coincide in the abdomen of these
woods. Leaves shadow-stitch my chest closed,
and the scabs in my lung peel off like bark –
patch after patch – until the whole fat of my
organ smooths into the bole of a rainbow
eucalyptus – molten-honey, nebula blue, neon
green ribboning down to the roots. The trunk
hardens, wrestles with the thunderstorms and
the tremble of chainsaws. Such a morning to
scour wounds – debride what's written in the
grime of fallen buds. Someone told me every
journey honours a roundtrip back to self. When
an outcry unfurls into courage and breath pulses
in concentric circles through a body that once
declined to mend. I sit in the gaps between
protruding roots, lean on the trunk's fluorescent
breadth, until my feet moss, moist with the
merciful soil, and what I fear folds into pleats
of leaves, and what's hurting subdues in the
wind's silk.

Laura Stanley

The Edge of the Pier

Fifteen and half-way under,
my skin translucening.
Deep down, not a breath of light.

I have been stitching small stones
in my clothes; mind blindly
tunneling down to a dirt bed.

You get a certain Arctic glaze
in your eye, she will tell me after.
A gravitational

magnetism. Her arms wrap
around me and she wrests me
away from the edge of the pier.

But how simple. How absolute!
A single step down. Floor – Gone.
Rush of a blown-out candle.

The sea murmurs, *lover, lover, lover.*
My mother holds me tight and tighter,
wants to push me back inside her.

Annie Hayter

Grandpa Hallelujah

Whenever a bird shits on me, I know it's not luck,
trailing whitely on my sleeve. It's my grandfather
in faecal form come to tell me what he thinks of
this new-fangled world I live in. If our life-lines
had intersected – my birth before his timely death –
he would have emptied hellfire into my babymouth,
scratched the sign of the beast onto the high forehead
that I grew, blooming from his daughter, fat-arsed,
chin sharp. In the mirror, the crook of his nose reminds
me how bent I am. It resembles a steeple. I disgust him
as my mother did, my skinny shoulders make bus-stops
for the devil to sit on. You could hide a woman's face
in them. Or two. He forbade love, sat with God, fishing
in the kitchen for sin. They debated ecumenical matters
long into the night, counted souls and money on the table.
He chewed life with much the same vigour as breakfast,
twenty times over, snow fickling at his heart's windows.
It never rains in heaven. He watched my mother as he'd
watch a thing with claws. In his home, she knew to obey
the two-square rule. Toilet paper was precious in the eyes
of the Lord. Waste was akin to murder. He tallied sections
of each roll, polished the leather shoes bought four decades
before, his little indulgence. His gaze lingers from a photo
on the mantelpiece, leathered with superstition. Mum kissed
the corpse, the feel of his cool cheek twitching on her lips.

Shivanee Ramlochan

All the Men Who Will Not Save You

The maker of missiles, the eroder of doubts
The quiet and triple-hipped starter of fires
The keeper of small bones and spiney growths

Him with a nesting doll full of hymens and sighs
Him with scarred hands cupped like satellites
Him in the night with your cunt in a crabcatcher

The undoer of welts, the unbelter of catechisms
The one with a face full of virtuous children
The geographer who cried, shaking out your maps

Them who do damage and never say sorry
Them as who damage you, sorrying in little drips
Them damagers with grasshopper blood sparkling
On their shirt cuffs in the bright and suspicious sun

I have always known I would devirgin myself best. Fist
full of pens, covers leaking neon, sour like cherries
sliced off the vine. A fistful of pens was my first lover.
I learned much later in life that a girl cannot deflower,
and so I plundered the language right out of myself, first
My fist a mess of ink and blood and gel and Barbie perfume
first, my nailbeds sour and puckered as the mouths of saints
Let no man say he came here first. Listen to him declaim
but know, I was the original breaker of me, I took, I kept.
I hoarded everything and locked the husbands out, first and last
of their names and stations, runners up in the violent arts.

When I am born again to this life you will not know me.
When I come startling into the world, how precious the cry
torn from lips like a holster, miniature guns spilling between
gumwork: I plan to come back here blazing, gelled in the saddle
ready to raze it down, ready to buck wild and bloody and fight.
If you hold me in your arms like a promise, I'll dissolve. If you
think you're going to make a bride of me, sweet boy, I'll melt.

Caroline Bird

The Frozen Aisle

"I'm in the mood," she said,
slotting in a pound
to free the trolley.
"What, here? In the Co-op?
Is there a toilet? Every aisle has CCTV?"
"No!" she said, activating
the sliding doors,
"In bed. Like normal humans."
"That sounds incredible,
let's grab essentials and run home."
"Onions," she said.
I flung a net of three in the cart.
Maybe this could be a game?
Supermarket Sweep foreplay?
"Lovely plums, eight for paaand!"
"What?"
"I'm a cockney market trader."
"We don't need plums."
She was staring intensely
at a probiotic low-fat yoghurt
with '100% Grass-Fed Cows'
written in gigantic font across the pot.
"Glass-fed," she said.
"What?"
"*Glass*-fed cows.
Wouldn't that be horrible?
Dripping blood from their big, trusting tongues?"
She held up a litre of semi-skimmed
with both hands like a bottle of wine.

"This reminds me of my childhood."
"It's milk."
"Am I safe?"
"Completely. Forever."
Just then, a crate of hot-cross buns
wheeled past and she burst into tears.
I tried to kiss her.
"Hang on a minute there, you little perv."
She ditched the trolley and ran
down the central aisle, shouting
breathily over her shoulder:
"And what was all that weird kinky dogging stuff
about Co-op toilets and CCTV?
This is all about urges for you, isn't it? Grubby urges?"
"No, it isn't." I ran after her.
"And now the desperation, running after me
like a stalker, holding a fucking stick
of garlic bread. I'm not aroused by garlic bread."
"Neither am I."
"So I guess we're at an impasse?"
"A what?"
"An impasse."
"We're not in a Greek tragedy."
"Aren't we?"
She shoved her phone in my face.
"4.5 Million Dead. Does that turn you on?"
"No, of course not."
My hands were shaking.
"We need space," she said, marching off,
clasping a jar of light mayonnaise
to her chest like an urn,

"…and we also need vegetable crisps."
Vegetable crisps.
The words yawned like a black hole,
sucking my eyes backwards
into my head until I saw
my own brain glowing
like a radioactive cauliflower.
"Don't rise to it,"
I whispered, but it was hopeless,
I'd risen like a body
from a tomb on Judgement Day,
shaking off the soil, queuing
with the other corpses in the aisles
between our stones, "What's going on?"
says one corpse. "I dunno," says another.
"Must be *time*," says another.
"Oh good," says another. "Oh shit,"
says another. "Don't worry," says another,
"anything's better than being down there."
"Yeah," I say, crunching the leaves
like vegetable crisps beneath the remains
of my feet. Then
the queue halts.
"False alarm. Back in the ground."
So, we all get back in our graves
and close our eyes
but we can't sleep now
we're too awake.

Gail Crowther

The Possession(s) of Sylvia Plath

Imagine walking into a room faced with mannequins straight from a de Chirico painting.

"Mother, mother, what illbred aunt / Or what disfigured and unsightly / Cousin did you so unwisely keep / Unasked to my christening, that she / Sent these ladies in her stead..." (Plath, 1988, 74).

Each mannequin is dressed in the clothes of Sylvia Plath. A blue, silken, embossed top, a daffodil-yellow dress, a swirly blue and white smock over a tartan kilt, and a brown dress with dainty bows at the waist. Each mannequin stands behind Plath's desk. Her olive-green Olivetti typewriter sits ready to use. To the left, her red oriental rug with a Victorian nursing chair and her glass-topped bamboo table. The objects of the dead. Melancholy objects. Books, galley-proofs, a tea-tray stained with smeary-ink, jewellery, annotated photographs, odd earrings, a copper hairband, a wallet, library cards, watches – time stopped, a thesaurus underlined and dog-eared. Such things, the thinginess of things.

But it is the clothes that fascinate. The shape, the texture, the colour, the outline of a body that is no longer there. I am in a sale room at Bonham's in London but feel I could be in Plath's closet at Court Green. The blue, silken top worn crossing the Atlantic for the last time, and for a New Year's Eve Party sixteen days before Nicholas was born. Or the plaid kilt featured in a photograph of Plath beaming outside Notre-Dame, Paris. The swirls and flowers of a blue smock top. It is like an intimate glimpse of her wardrobe, the still-vibrant colours of the fabric, the crisp cotton, the soft silk, the thick wool. Each crease, pleat, fold, smoothed by fingers. Zips and buttons, done and undone. The headless mannequin is a poor stand-in for the body that should be there, that was once there, that will never be there again.

Objects of the dead – how do we deal with them and what they do they mean? Margaret Gibson refers to them as melancholy objects, those things that are left behind when someone had gone. Things that we use to negotiate mourning and loss, which open discourses on death and absence. Each object left behind by the dead is inextricably linked to the biography of the owner and the "death of an individual creates a biographical-historical separation between a specific subject and their possessions" (2010, 2). But as Gibson points out, the space that this separation creates is filled with a number of things. Most importantly, a symbolic continuity. The objects and possessions act as some sort of spectral stand-in for the absent person. They are still referred to as belonging to their former owner ("Plath's dresses"). They show us the missing shape and outline, they trigger memories of the vanished body. But the *type* of memories triggered must surely be different if we knew the dead person. A coat casually left over the back of a chair may still smell of a lost, loved one, the bodily imprint in the material familiar and comforting. But a dress once worn by someone we never knew cannot trigger memories of familiarity. It can only remind us that a body once used to be there and is now gone. It can show us the outline, the shape, the nuances of a person and our imagination conjures up the rest.

At the point of death, the objects move across private and personal spaces into public spaces and commercial domains. These objects of which I write were, after all, in a Bonham's sale with a charge, a very large charge. Finally, Gibson wonders whether there are notions of magic taking place too – the idea that one is getting closer to an aura, or an essence imbued in an object that has touched the body of the lost person (do we imagine those spectral traces that Plath left behind?).

"…What is it / Survives, grieves / So…" (Plath, 1988, 110). When we touch something that she touched or wore, are we trying to capture some bodily echo or reverberation from the past?

The status of these clothes is different to, say, a poem manuscript, a letter or a journal. Each of these items have their own unique intimacy, yet the latter feel concerned with Plath's interiority. What she thought, what she observed, what her creative mind was exploding onto the page, how she was communicating the inside of her head into textual form. Clothes though, are different. They may feature *in* some of Plath's writing, but they concern themselves with Plath's exteriority, how she chose to present her sense of identity to the world, or the literal embodied presentation of her-self. Clothes say so much about us. Their make and quality, the colour and style. Plath favoured well-made, rather expensive clothes in a variety of colours. Each piece felt valuable, durable, and impervious to time. No faded colours, no tears or stains. Remarkable, given their age and how well-travelled they were in Plath's lifetime alone. Their posthumous life is more of a mystery. Where have they been all these years? Some clothing was shipped back across the Atlantic to Plath's mother and distributed among family and friends. But the life-after-death history of the clothes in the Bonham's sale room is unknown. They move through history as material remnants of a life once lived. Hockey, Komaromy, and Woodthorpe (2010) speculate upon "the ways in which an individual's personal belongings, their clothing, shoes, watch and jewellery, not only constitute part of their personhood, but also, once they have died, assume enhanced agency as residual fragments which can stand for that individual in their entirety." (10).

These residual fragments tell us much about Plath as a woman. We know that she was a person who loved to buy clothes and we know that she loved the way she could present herself to the outside world using certain dresses, skirts, tops, hosiery to make herself feel better. There is much pleasure to be had in fashion and what Plath often thought of as the trappings of femininity, what she described in a 1962 interview for the British Council as, the "lares and penates" of a woman's life. But also, the self-care and confidence that feeling good in certain clothes can give us.

During 1957-1958, that difficult teaching year at Smith College, despite dreading classes and facing her students, Plath wrote in her journal, "I am sure I teach better in certain dresses whose colors & textures war not against my body & my thought." (Plath, 2000, 335). The idea that clothes give us confidence is not new of course, but Plath often linked what she wore to how productive she could be. When she took her swish clothes to Paris as a Cambridge student, the colours and texture seemed to seep into her very mood, delighting in herself for herself since she was alone as she walked the city at night, "Dressed in black velvet and felt most chic in mackintosh, ironically, because of its swaggery cut; nonchalant, debonair, yet un peu triste because no one was there to chariot me." (Plath, 2000, 558). She revelled in new, good quality clothes that made her feel feminine and made her body feel desirable, "I dressed, conscious of color and the loveliness of being thin and feeling slink, swank and luxurious in good fits and rich materials. For the first time put on my red silk stockings with red shoes – they feel amazing...I can't stop looking..." (Plath, 2000, 379). She uses sensuous language to describe the shifting reds and roses of her glowing stockings. In contrast, at home, she felt comfortable in older, everyday clothes that gave her quieter, less showy feelings of pleasure, often her familiar tweeds of purply-blue worn when she was pregnant with Frieda, "Felt warm in my tweeds, pleasantly fat-stomached. The baby is a pleasure to dream on." (Plath, 2000, 526). And like many of us, lamenting when she didn't have the money to buy what she wanted, "The desire also for money which I am miserly about, not buying clothes nor frills, although I could go wild doing so – startling dresses & frivolously colored shoes to match." (Plath, 2000, 375).

As well as highlighting her mood and creativity, Plath used clothes to transform. In 1962 after living in Devon and the birth of Nicholas, Plath felt she had somehow lost her sense of style. When a teenage neighbour visited for afternoon tea, Plath wrote in her journal, "I managed a girdle & stockings & heels and felt a new person." (Plath, 2000, 634). But the word "managed" is revealing. In the autumn of 1962 when her marriage had broken down, this is when Plath really went for the break-up makeover, getting her hair cut and styled for the first time in years, "I had my fringe cut…in the most fashionable style --- high on top, curling down round the ears --- and kept my long coronet in the back. It looks fabulous…" (Plath, 2018, 898). Then, she spent gift money on a clothes shopping spree in Exeter; a camel suit she had seen in *Vogue*, a matching camel sweater, a black sweater, a black and blue tweed skirt, a duck-green cardigan, and a red wool skirt. Once again, she uses the expression, feeling like "a new woman" transforming from the old into the new, with an exciting, independent life ahead. The transformation continued late into the year when she moved to London in December and wrote with glee, "I have found the most fantastic store --- Dickens & Jones which knocks Harrods out of the window. I spent the rest of Mrs P's clothes money & feel & look like a million…" (Plath, 2018, 940). She describes buying a Florence-Italy blue and white velvet overblouse, a brown velvet Italian shirt, black fake-fur toreador pants, a metallic blue and black French top, and a black velvet skirt.

This delight in splurging money on clothes went as far back as her student days. An expenditure list from Smith College shows that in the year 1952-1953, Plath spent $65 on books, $15 on food, $55 on transport, but an impressive $310 on clothes.

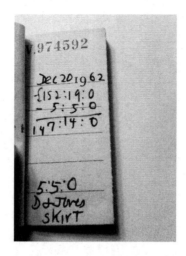

When we encounter the clothes of Sylvia Plath, we encounter her joy. She is no longer with us, but she leaves behind so many gifts. The astonishing legacy of her writing, the remains of household possessions, rugs, jewellery, trinkets, painted furniture, library books, and stopped watches. But her clothes – her clothes – radiate her absent body. They radiate her love of life and hope for the future. They tell us of her happy times and her delight in their colour, texture, feel. They tell us that when she wore them she felt wonderful, whether she was strolling the streets of Paris or London, or simply taking tea at home in Devon.

After Sylvia, let us remember her joy in the way that clothes transformed her and her view of life. In a November 1962 letter written from Devon just before she moved to London, she declared that she was leaving all her old clothes behind and taking only her new, spectacular ones. "I want," she wrote defiantly, "my life to begin over from the skin out." (Plath, 2018, 912).

Works cited:
Sylvia Plath, *Collected Poems* (London: Faber and Faber, 1988).
Margaret Gibson, "Death and the Transformation of Objects and Their Value" *Thesis Eleven*, 2010.
Jenny Hockey, Carol Komaromy, & Kate Woodthorpe, *The Matter of Death: Space, Place and Materiality* (London: Palgrave Macmillan, 2010).
Sylvia Plath, *The Journals of Sylvia Plath* (London: Faber and Faber, 2000).
Sylvia Plath, *The Letters of Sylvia Plath Volume II 1956-1963* (London: Faber and Faber, 2018).
All photographs © Gail Crowther.

WOMANHOOD

Rebecca Goss

When it feels hot, that rage against me

will I tell you of the pitch-black mile
    walked with cidery mouths, our hair
  flushed in occasional headlight, throats singing

Sweet Child O' Mine, a distance increasing
    from men we left at the pub, too old, too
  frightening when they did react to the early

curve of our bodies. My mother elsewhere
    in the starlit hinterland, just the lane knowing
  how to hold us, its chorus of night creatures.

The collapse into a bedroom, the joint
    a shared firefly at our lips, clothes strewn,
  soon sleeping like children. I will understand

your need to be away from me and with girls,
    girls I want to wake now, pull from
  the men they chose, pull from their tumble-dried sheets,

become a multitude storming under stars, sky crackling
    at the sight of us, all the promises re-rising
  in our throats, needing each other like fire.

Victoria Kennefick

O Brigid, O Exalted One, Listen to my Plea as I Celebrate You

(whispers)

Remember
she is only the size of a strawberry seed,
of a bristle on a toothbrush.
Tiny, tadpole-like
with a tail
growing –

Flame-haired, you are in the damp grass, Brigid,
your pale hands cradle me, cup me like water.
I lick across your palms, molecules of me expecting
to reassemble a newborn body, fluid and fresh.
Goddess of wells, Goddess of wombs
and words and the first light of morning,
carry me to where I can spring forth.
        Pour me into the stream so I flow,
        use me to cool the red-hot
        iron of your smithing – all sunlight and fire.
        Help me to rise like you though I fall,
        to surge through it all –
        gush over dry stone. Heal me,
        let me keep this seed safe, deliver it
wrapped in your cloak, fully-grown to the earth.
I don't want to keen anymore, my throat
dry from the emptiness in my arms.
I don't want to give this one back. I drop
coins in the river, leave an apple at its lip
and on the bank the bread that failed to rise.
I will cross and recross myself with grass and sticks –

three armed and ready for battle with whatever
wants to take my babies from me.
Now you're wading in with me and mine, Brigid.
The red line of dawn slaps blue water,
a confluence, and you will hold us all
in flame and wave,
won't you?

Angela Cleland

Pineapple (Objects in a portrait I)

In this context, the pineapple
represents death, and death represents
obscurity. In Victorian times
mourning women who found themselves
smirking upon mention of the deaths of their husbands
would bind the skin of a pineapple
beneath their corsets to give themselves
an appropriately pained expression.
The dual action of the rough peel
and the acidic juice was reported to have,
on occasion, caused permanent scarring.

I can see that you don't believe me.
Perhaps you've never eaten too much pineapple
or had too much husband,
or come to the realisation
that the smooth feeling on your lips
which follows tropical over-indulgence
is a gloss of your own dissolved skin cells
mourning their past life as something protective.
Perhaps you've never had to wear
your own discomfort to keep yourself in check.
Forget it. It's only a painting.

Sarah Corbett

Prick

The hawthorn stabs me through the back of the hand
hits a vein and retreats. By evening, the swelling

is a seethe of cells, nerves prickling in my wrist.
I sit with the discomfort, the welt a swirl of skin

taut around the puncture, and life draws near.
How many years I've looked from this window,

the view of trees and rooftops and hill now humps
and twiggy fingers. It's a full moon night, a blue flood,

a tenderness of light in the garden, the branches
trimmed last year a mass of inch-long needles,

no mention yet of buds or flowers. As girls we sewed
our fingertips, passing a needle under the epidermis,

thread following thread until we'd looped a whole hand
like a cat's cradle, the subtle throb, the ache and tug

we delighted in, the bolster of flesh beneath, lightly pierced.
Afterwards the pads would flake and peel, flushed pink

and new. We were *testing, testing* – mushroom clouds
off Bikini Atoll, the long-dripped flaps from the child

running and crying in the photograph – trying pain on
for size, the needle and ice cube piercing of ears and

noses, matches lit and smothered in our mouths; snakebite,
half bottle of whiskey, daily bottle of vodka. The puncture

heals but leaves its mark. How tough touch is, and how
we persist, holding our hand to the flame until the burn.

Clara Rosarius

The Collectors

you learn that ravens steal the silver things:
the still-sticky-spoon on the picnic blanket,
pebbles shined by sweater sleeves, a loose nail,
a lost paperclip in the potted knotweeds.
you learn what it means to be dirty, that
grass-stains don't wash out, that each month
you bleed the punishment for an empty womb,
that shame is expected. you learn the joy of momentary things,
figs, covers from the dryer, the smell of unwanted
Christmas trees on the curb. you learn to desire
the beating of egg-whites until they are stiff, the beached
body in the road, that when you breathe on dandelions
they are already dead. you don't learn how to live,
wanting to be picked, fearing the nest.
you don't learn how to tell a mother
why you too are drawn to silver things,
but not the soft spoon, or the tipped coin by the gutter;
that instead you are sometimes drawn to the blade.

Sally Baker

My Life as a Tulip

I'm all underskirts and can-can frills in the online picture.
Hand-packed on a production line of women,
I arrive in a twist of brown paper, bone-white, a late bloomer.

It's unbearable then to be buried, covered in winter blankets.
My roots stretch into darkness studded with planetary dust.
In my restless nights I hallucinate through fever.

Every freeze and thaw is as bleak as the first.
After the harshest time, vernalised under permafrost,
light comes, with a new sound like a charm bracelet

shaken free from the earth, or an early blackbird's song.
Even if I'm broken, mosaic virus shot through my petals like ink,
disease might make me rare and beautiful,

like *Semper Augustus*. I'd be as valuable as a mansion
surrounded by orchards. Everything is still possible.
When I ascend in my satin dress, I'll blaze.

Merrie Joy Williams

Snap

This is for little black girls who showed up for class photos in dresses their mothers chose. Miniature dresses like their mamas wore to dead-end jobs, sermons which vilified them, obligatory birthday parties where they'd end up serving food, waiting for overdue compliments. Dresses asymmetric as their marriages, in the style of countries they were never taken on holiday. The lemon yellows of Mexico, the burnt orange ruches of Spain. Or else brown and beige, muted as vexed tongues, as if the bodice's flowers had rotted on the stem, from having never been picked for them. And, in Autumn, the leaves on the sleeves had fallen like tears, for divorces late as periods, whispering as they fluttered, *'Oh no – another year!'*

Little black girls who were someone's late period. Who showed up for class photos in dresses that their mothers chose and poses that the teachers selected, modelled in triplicate, in front of neat privets. Compliant smiles, faint, frozen lips purporting sadness as restraint. Tempers éven as 9 to 5 weekdays – then more work after hours, unpaid, unpaid. Farrah Fawcett hair, supposedly flyaway, but stiff as stone to fingertips. Little black girls who'd grow to sacrifice their scalps to relaxer kits, the burning fire of the lye, the lie, whilst courtesy Aunts cried: *'Wait as long as you can bear it!'* – before they'd wash it out for them. As if womanhood were an endurance test.

Black girls who were someone's late periods, but showed up on time for photos, in dresses that their mothers chose, poses their teachers selected, rows that their gender dictated: sat at the front, knees together, hands in laps. Then boys stood behind, arranged by height, barely a smile between them. Then the boys at the back, stood on the bench like kings, already learning women stand behind them, no matter how successful. Little black girls whose knees were slathered in Vaseline, their partings with Dixie Peach. Or whose hair was too short to pull into pigtails, but still wore the dress, yanking down the hem as if guarding a secret.

Mona Arshi

Queen Kreon watches on

*When deep inside you there is a loaded gun,
how can you have God? Kabir*

I was half asleep and heavy with a first child
    when the carcass was carried inside and inspected.

    The ceremony began, the King leaned over
the deer's body and placed a hand on his heart.

He had no more need for pelts, but what
    could be holier than being so close to a

    warm thing cooling in front of your eyes.
The cup bearer came forward and anointed it.

The air changed then – the Gods were in the great hall.
    The chatter stopped; the animal was emptied out.

    Its gutting reminding me of a fleshy plum,
its stone deftly pushed out with expert fingers.

I hadn't expected it to be so precise…so tidy.
    I wanted something operatic, for the dark blood

    to pool onto the floor, but the men
didn't even have to wipe themselves down.

Her eyelashes were fair, golden even.
    I wanted to nurse her, to put her on my breast

and touch the small feint patch on her jaw.
But I couldn't move. I shouldn't have been there.

I know now the Gods would have followed
my scent to the shadows where I stood,

they would have found me sandal-less,
   quiet, the boy stirring inside me as

I watched them hold her vascularised heart
which had stopped in the middle of a dream.

Karen McCarthy Woolf

Ariel

/because an angel, a deity commands attention/chivalry, or /deference/
even—I mean I can't believe she's still getting away with it/

ffs everyone knows *it's* there, and they're still running with *well it wasn't
quite so beyond the pale in nineteen sixty-two* although that's the year MLK
first had a fucking dream: yes, profanity as an interruption to the sacred,
that's how it feels, when you're not Lady/[fucking]

Godiva with milk-white skin sat naked, straddling your mount, or
sometimes, sat coyly side-saddle, depending on the artist, your long,
straight hair arrowing in the wind behind you—that's how it feels to
come across *it*, unexpectedly, while trying to fathom the substanceless
blue, yes, and that's why, tb/h, I never really checked for Hemingway,
another American who also knew exactly what he was doing with syntax,
metaphor, archetypes etc, and remembering/

it, the casual, ruthless violence when its sleek head pops out of the water;
but my job is to turn a blind eye, God, there's something so un/

just about the critical reception, which still chooses to avert its [   ] gaze/
knowing full well that most [   ] readers will also look away, as one does
in the bright, moon face of something awful or ugly, and I say this/

lovingly, as a mother/might because I want you, dear [   ] reader, to
feel what I feel, so you too can grow, become stronger, be resilient and
generous as you acknowledge yet rise above *it* so as to savour and learn
from canonical genius, sacrificing your own dreams and opportunity to
occupy vicarious hero status and those of your brother, father, sister, son,
daughter, aunt, cousin, uncle in the process, albeit fleetingly, because it
happens in the blink of a

/*Nigger-eye/d berry* so the whole thing vibrates in a moment of impossible stasis, especially when you then read the words *brown—arc—neck—catch—dark—Hook—black—sweet—blood—Hauls* in such/ominous/

proximity that the whole poem/quivers, as a body at the end of a/rope might/shudder and/twitch and that body could be your [   ]body—it's an/ unpleasant proposition this needling, this mewling insistence/

vindicated only by its enduring necessity, this/

work we keep on doing, these correctives, when all we want is also to be/

exultant as a glitter of sea/yearning, freely, for the/azure

Ruth Fainlight

Ashes and Dust

As water saturates everything
dust penetrates everywhere,
sifts between each page of a book
(and there are so many books),
sinks into the layered fabrics
of folded blouses and nightgowns,
hangs in the air like a veil of smoke
from a burning house. Catastrophe.

Pain and tears. So many deaths. Ordeals
of fire and water, dust and ashes;
infanticide, suicide.
Wife, mistress and her daughter:
he lived through it all, hardened
into survival. An idol,
awesome, hated and adored.

From childhood, that compulsion,
starting with her father's death.
She wanted to know how it felt
and what it meant, to follow him
wherever he went. Three days' coma.
She was found in the space under the porch,
snails' slime-trails across her face and legs.

What was it that reminded her
of her father? Reader, she married him
to find out. Those hearts and flowers
she painted on every piece
of furniture in the nursery
were part of her paternal heritage.
Not until she told her husband to go
could she escape their influence,
become another sacred monster.

Ashes to ashes and dust
to dust. Now both of them are dead.
But they are resurrected,
identities defined, restored
as monster and idol:
sacred, hated, awesome and adored.
Their words still vividly alive.

Jane Commane

She said I needed to do the work of anger

After 'The Munich Mannequins'

And I sat among the branches of the tree I had
pruned so long with my silences and hurts and searched
for the fruit I had grown, the little waxy nubs of yellow

hardened by all the things a woman must not say,
their flesh bitter and the pips catching in the throat
and what rose up in me wasn't the sickly swell

of fury but the ferment of everything I had forced
down: the fizzing moon of all my sorrys, the lichen
that bleached and spread snowlike and hid me,

the hard press of panic that slid its flagstone over the roots
of me, stopped my words with dried leaves and left me,
a tree branching bone-brittle and mannequin still,

in this fumigated orchard where brimstone blanches the bud
and blows cool on the white-hot core of the star at the centre
of an apple sliced through with one clean cross of the knife.

So I do the work of anger, of joy. I do the work of love
for what good would come of these flowers of sulphur left to
bloom until even the heartwood of me is crystalline.

Heather Clark

"Prisoner & Jailor, / Perfectly parabled": The October Poems' Art of Escape

At the end of James Joyce's 1916 novel, *A Portrait of the Artist as a Young Man*, Stephen Dedalus leaves his home in Ireland for an exile's life in Europe. He is certain that if he stays, the Irish church and state will kill his artistic spirit. He refuses to serve either institution: this famous flight was, in Joyce's memorable phrase, Stephen's *non serviam*.

James Joyce was one of Sylvia Plath's literary heroes. Her college notebooks are full of illuminating notes on his novels, and she chose to marry on June 16, Bloomsday. Like Joyce and Stephen, Plath too felt the oppressive weight of a conservative society's expectations, and the danger of fulfilling them. Plath came of age in 1950s Cold War America at a time when women were expected to sublimate their professional ambitions to a husband and children. Plath wanted a family, but she also wanted to become a great writer. She had a strong sense of her destiny, and searched for the right conditions in America that might allow her to fulfil her calling. At Smith College she was a star student, nurtured by caring professors. But outside the college gates, opportunities hid dark traps: boyfriends dismissed her desire to write; an internship at *Mademoiselle* magazine precipitated a breakdown; even her Smith College commencement speaker, Adlai Stevenson, urged her graduating class to become housewives. Plath, like Stephen, took flight. She left America first in 1955 and again in 1959, never to return. The conditions for women in her adopted home of England were hardly better than they were in America, but in England, at least, she enjoyed the lonely freedom of the exile.

Plath also left behind suffocating conceptions of womanhood in her poems. We might think of *Ariel* as Plath's own *non serviam*, for in these poems, Plath rejected the anodyne, decorous constraints on language she felt had limited women poets before her, just as she rejected sentimental, cosseted, "womanly" themes. Plath understood that breaking free from demeaning expectations meant breaking through her own layers of self-doubt and, perhaps, internalised misogyny. Several of her best poems explore the dynamic of female imprisonment and escape from an oppressive double, the judgements of other women, or the control of men. This was a theme she returned to again and again in poems that refused to play nice.

Months before she embarked upon her *Ariel* poems, Plath wrote 'In Plaster', about a patient recovering at a hospital in a full body cast. The poem speaks to women's experience of freedom and imprisonment, increasingly on Plath's mind as her marriage took a dark turn in the early months of 1961. The poem's speaker-patient inhabits the "old yellow" body imprisoned beneath the clean alabaster cast, which the speaker describes as "superior" and "one of the real saints." "I shall never get out of this! There are two of me now," Plath writes. Plath here explores the "double" theme that had fascinated her since her Smith College days, when she had written a thesis about the double in Dostoyevsky's work. But 'In Plaster' sounds a new note of feminist protest. The poem expresses a divided condition that Plath knew well, and would have been familiar to many women in 1961. The plaster cast represents the outer self that conformed to conservative standards of femininity dictated by society. This self is at odds with the more authentic inner self that secretly rebelled from such strictures. The speaker's cast – a literal bodily prison – is a metaphor for the societal repressions that keep women's true emotions and desires encased. The cast, Plath says, "was shaped just the way I was" but was "unbreakable and with no complaints." It represents the perfect, selfless woman who sacrifices her own desires to serve others; it is "the best of nurses," full of "tidiness," "calmness," and "patience." The speaker within the cast, on the other hand, is none of these things: she is "ugly and hairy," with offensive, possibly dirty, "habits." The speaker trapped within feels buried alive: "Living with her was like living with my own coffin."

The emotional toll of living a divided life, especially as an ambitious woman in the 1950s and 60s, is on full display in this witty but unsettling poem. It is a theme that had a prominent place in the novel Plath was about to begin: *The Bell Jar*. Indeed, Ted Hughes later suggested, in an unpublished poem, that 'In Plaster' was the key to understanding the character of Esther Greenwood and the *Ariel* poems that followed:

There you are: Prisoner & Jailor,
Perfectly parabled.
And for the first time (not quite the first)
The prisoner speaks the speech
And stays centre-stage
The jailor, no more voice than a straitjacket
Dangling on a tree, never after
Got a word in.

Hughes finished the section, "Ariel was at large." He felt 'In Plaster' marked the point when Plath stopped pretending to be the "good girl" that society demanded – a role that was fiercely at odds with her ambition to become a great writer, an ambition that would have been seen as immodest and self-aggrandising for a woman at this time. 'In Plaster' exhibits a steely determination on the speaker's part to break free from the saintly façade imposed upon her, and to honour the authentic voice within. This escape was something that Hughes had been encouraging for years, and which Plath herself had been attempting since at least 1959, when she had written about her longing to break free from what she called the "glass caul" in her journal. She wanted to shed her overreliance on poetic form, but encoded within this desire was a more general need to break from similarly "encasing" feminine rules that encouraged self-censorship and subordination. These were the rules of a patriarchal society, designed to keep women from becoming great writers – or indeed great leaders of any kind. These rules kept women powerless and "in their place"; they were, as Plath suggests in her poem, an invisible, immobilising cast. 'In Plaster' announces a rebellion: at the end, Plath's speaker declares herself victorious, saying, "I'm collecting my strength; one day I shall manage without her." And indeed, Plath's time in the hospital, which brought back memories of her earlier mental hospital stays, inspired her to begin and quickly finish *The Bell Jar* – a novel which explores several of the same themes in 'In Plaster'.

Plath's unapologetic boldness and rebellion from traditional modes of womanhood animates much of *Ariel*, especially the poems she wrote in October, 1962 – the month Hughes left Plath, their children, and their home in Devon. October was a time of heartbreak, but Plath also saw

59

an opportunity to grow and become more independent in the wake of Hughes's leavetaking. In the poems she wrote that month, speakers make their escape.

The first poems Plath wrote that October were 'The Detective' and 'The Courage of Shutting Up'; both portray female speakers as survivors of violence. In the latter poem, a tongue in danger of being "cut out" is finally unleashed to speak the truth: "it is dangerous." Plath's poems, likewise, will perform this "dangerous" unleashing as Plath herself refuses to remain silent, especially in the wake of her husband's betrayal. Plath's speakers in *Ariel* will blast sentimental feminine ideas. They have nothing left to lose, and everything to gain, from speaking their truths. Hughes's departure was the catalyst for this new tone, which had first announced itself with 'Zoo Keeper's Wife' ("I entered your bible, I boarded your ark"), but the themes of rebirth, resurrection, transcendence, motherhood, and depression had been part of Plath's oeuvre for years. Now, a more determined rebelliousness and flagrant disregard for propriety propelled the poems aloft. Plath would no longer "shut up." The poems of *Ariel* insist upon being heard, foreshadowing the critic Maggie Nelson's later sense that "the injunction to behave appropriately … is but a death knell for art-making, especially for women."

Plath referred to the next group of poems she wrote that October as "the Bee sequence" in her letters. 'The Bee Meeting', 'The Arrival of the Bee Box', 'Stings', 'The Swarm', and 'Wintering' were based upon her experience of beekeeping in Devon during the summer of 1962, and they also drew upon the legacy of her father, Otto Plath, whose magnum opus was his academic study *Bumblebees and Their Ways*. The poems speak of power and powerlessness, vulnerability and strength. 'Stings' and 'Wintering' are the most personal of the sequence; in 'Stings' the speaker compares herself to the queen bees in her hives. No longer will she accept subordination: "I / Have a self to recover, a queen." She will have her revenge on the feminine domestic:

> Now she is flying
> More terrible than she ever was, red
> Scar in the sky, red comet
> Over the engine that killed her –
> The mausoleum, the wax house.

Here Plath implies that "the engine that killed her" is the house itself, which has become a "mausoleum." The speaker escapes in flight – an iconic Plathian trope. In 'Wintering', the last poem in Plath's original ordering of *Ariel*, the speaker ponders the bees she keeps in her cellar. "They have got rid of the men," Plath writes. The speaker wonders, "Will the hive survive...?" and suggests her own freedom at the poem's end, "The bees are flying. They taste the spring."

'Fever 103°', finished on October 20, interrogates metaphorically imprisoning feminine symbols and archetypes. Plath begins almost philosophically – "Pure? What does it mean?" – aware of the myriad ways this question (and answer) has limited women's lives. Plath plays with the trope of purity through the ages – particularly men's demand for it – as the speaker hallucinates and imagines herself a virgin whose sullied "selves" ("old whore petticoats") dissolve as she ascends to Paradise. Plath treats the symbols of "pure" femininity with a deflating irony as the speaker imagines herself surrounded by roses, kisses, and cherubim, "By whatever these pink things mean." As in 'The Tour' and 'Lesbos', Plath mocks the oppressive trappings of female propriety and sentimentality – though here, the send-up is more exuberant. Even as Plath satirises the idea of purity, the speaker's longing for it gives the poem an ambiguous edge.

In 'The Tour', completed on October 25, Plath indeed shows that she has gathered her strength, and is managing "without her." This time, the metaphorical jailor is a woman poet who, Plath felt, had tried to silence her. In the poem, the speaker flaunts her messy house – and by extension, her messy, rebellious lifestyle – to a "maiden aunt" based on the poet Marianne Moore. Plath had once looked to Moore as a mentor, but she had upset Plath by calling her poems "bitter, frost-bitten, burnt out, averse" in a 1962 letter to Plath's Knopf editor. Now Plath was striking back. "I am bitter? I'm averse?" the speaker proclaims, after warning her visitor against getting too close to her appliances (the frost-box makes "millions of needly glass cakes!" and the furnace burns the speaker's hair off). Plath, a model hausfrau, uses the metaphor of the clean house to mock oppressive feminine standards of soul-deadening propriety. The speaker's house is messy and she meets her visitor in "slippers and housedress with no lipstick!" The exclamation points emphasise an extremity of emotion that might just be unseemly. Plath's speaker doesn't care whether she makes the correct impression on this conservative dowager. 'The Tour' is Plath's message to Moore, whose persona and work she mocks as chilly, oppressive, and life-denying. (The fact that Moore had asked Hughes to omit certain poems that used sexual language from *The Hawk in the Rain* only fuelled Plath's indignation.)

'The Tour' was written three and a half months before the publication of *The Feminine Mystique*, but it expresses a similar exhaustion with – and rebellion from – traditional mores of femininity. It also espouses a rawer, more taboo aesthetic that both Plath and Hughes, as well as Robert Lowell, Anne Sexton, and Al Alvarez, had embraced. In this sense, 'The Tour' itself stands as a fitting example of the Nietzschean brand of philosophy that animates *Ariel*: these poems would embrace freedom of expression and disavow puritanism. They would refuse to submit or please. Plath knew their impact would be shocking and revolutionary, as she hints in 'The Tour' when the speaker tells her visitor to "toddle on home to tea in your flat hat" while she enjoys "Lemon tea and earwig biscuits – creepy-creepy. / You'd not want that." By highlighting her speaker's "weirdnesses," Plath diminishes Moore's aesthetic and emboldens her own. Plath here lays down the gauntlet: nothing less than the direction of modern poetry is at stake.

If 'The Tour' is, in part, about escaping the invisible cast of the feminine domestic, Lady Lazarus – a corpse – escapes the oppressive beauty standards of the female body altogether, and revels in bodily corruption. She has come back from the dead before and now taunts her audience, the "peanut-crunching crowd," who has paid to see her die again. Plath uses grotesque imagery – maggots, eye pits, bad breath – to parody the "big strip tease" Lady Lazarus performs under this surreal big-top. Lady Lazarus's face is "Bright as a Nazi lampshade"; later in the poem, she dissolves into a "cake of soap, / A wedding ring, / A gold filling." Plath's seemingly blithe use of these images for their shock-value angered critics, and still cause controversy today. But the poem ought not to be dismissed. Its sophisticated use of irony and performance turn the mirror back upon the reader: Plath asks *us* to question our own attraction to extremities of death and destruction. After all, an audience has paid handsomely to see this living corpse and Nazi victim perform. Plath's message may be closer to that of Susan Sontag, who famously questioned the morality of viewing Holocaust photographs. That Lady Lazarus is presented as a victim of fascism is no accident: Plath here makes a connection between fascism, itself an extreme form of masculine violence, and the spectacle of violence against women. Plath wrote most of 'Lady Lazarus' during the most intense period of the Cuban Missile Crisis, October 22 to October 27, 1962, which may explain the anger toward men who were, less than two decades after the Second World War, once again steering the world toward apocalypse.

'Lady Lazarus' treats the confessional impulse, too, with deep irony and cynicism. Plath's invocation of the strip tease trope invokes pornography, but it is not physical arousal the audience has paid for – rather, Plath suggests, it is the equally satisfying spectacle of watching a woman fall apart. Plath understood that a woman's fall from grace was a form of misogynist entertainment as old as time. Both Plath, as she writes, and Lady Lazarus, as she performs, are aware of this sexist dynamic, which is perhaps why Lady Lazarus promises at the poem's end to "rise" like a Phoenix out of the ash and "eat men like air" – a line that seems to pun on the idea of an empty threat. The revenge fantasy is just that; Plath draws attention to women's powerlessness in the face of brute masculine violence epitomised by fascism. Like 'Edge', 'Lady Lazarus' satirises the idea that a dead woman is "perfected," and gives the impression of having been written posthumously. It is as if Plath foresaw her own literary legacy as a confessional poet, and predicts her readers' voracious appetite for the most sensational, death-ridden details from her life.

'Purdah' seemingly picks up where 'Lady Lazarus' leaves off, with the promise to destroy men. Written during the same week as 'Lady Lazarus', 'Purdah' rehearses the story of Clytemnestra's murder of Agamemnon from Clytemnestra's point of view. The end of 'Purdah' conjures the famous murder: "The shriek in the bath." Plath's largely sympathetic portrayals of traditionally reviled Classical heroines such as Clytemnestra and Medea (in 'Edge') were innovative. In her poems, they are given the chance to explain, if not justify, their acts of vengeance against the men who betrayed them. Plath speaks for these and other women who have been silenced by history, misogyny, self-doubt, or brute force. In the October poems, the prisoner now "speaks the speech," as Hughes put it, while the jailor looks on, powerless to stop her.

Works Cited:

References to ' "Prisoner & Jailor, / Perfectly parabled": The October Poems' Art of Escape' by Heather Clark

All quotes from Sylvia Plath's poetry are from: Sylvia Plath, *Collected Poems*, ed. Ted Hughes. London: Faber & Faber, 1981.

"There you are: Prisoner & Jailor": Ted Hughes, "Trial Sequence," British Library Add MS 99883/1/1.

"the injunction to behave appropriately": Maggie Nelson, *The Art of Cruelty: A Reckoning*. New York: W.W. Norton, 2011), p. 246.

MAGIC

Pascale Petit

Swarm

That day the
swarm hung in my tiny East
London garden, under the stump of
the buddleia – my tomcat on the compost
beneath, his green eyes mesmerised, his ears
cocked at the roar. I padded around, staring through
windows, then lay in the bath, the louvre open, and
the water shivered as if the bursting bubbles were water-
bees tattooing their queen code into my skin. I dared not
approach the blossoming bomb. It was as if aliens had landed,
crystalline cyborgs whose pheromones issued instructions –
humans keep out – their old queen at the core, sperm stored inside
her from a hundred drones, while scouts danced directions to
her new hive, vibrating scent-trails with their abdomens. Each
bee's five eyes glowed with maps of possible homes. As if all
my homes, even the children's home, were stuffed into that long
hot mirror-ball. All the waggle dance of my life. On the second
day I saw that the swarm had grown a tail, unwinding the ball
in a trail of smoke, a coiled Z drifting away through a passage
like a wormhole. Then it swerved and a bronze blizzard filled
the sky. I thought how earth's mantle is riddled with tunnels
and the air sings with turbulent streams. Then it was gone, and
men came to clear the collapsed shed away, razing the jasmine
and its ghost hordes where now, at the core, bivouacked in
my amygdala, lay my triumph at first pronouncing my name.
How the children of the orphanage had pressed around
me in a writhing mass as they pushed me towards the
window and its pollen-gilded warrior. I was the girl who
had closed my hand around a bee – that pause when
everything was possible as vowels brushed their
wings against my palm before the last syllable
barbed. But it didn't matter, I was
beyond harm. I held my name
in my fist.

Jonah Corren

Scavengers

It only looked like a deer for a few days. Steadily,
deliberately, it was unworked, unstitched like
old curtains, and distributed evenly: a napkin, a skirt,
a tea-cosy. Dusk imitated the flicker of frames, a timelapse
spilling the deer's outlines like lentils from the split side
of a paper bag. The slow clunk of every car, the weathering,
the descent of buzzards and magpies, unpainting as
performance. It wasn't supposed to be enjoyed like this. The
front row seats. The SUV tiptoeing through the undergrowth,
with all the subtlety of a swarm of jackdaws. We provided the
stage, the camera, the full house – they provided the show.
Such a marvel too, to speed over concrete glistening with
finality, tyres chattering applause like front-set eyes, glowing
from deep beyond the trees.

Ian Humphreys

shadow
shifter

and after that I turned into a jay
        sloughing   mole pelt
                when the puffball blew
    its dark magic
        onto my tongue

            my screams shook trees naked
        and the red moon rose
                                through me
            like fever   cobalt wings bared
        I was swept up
by a leaf blizzard to the peaks of

            a familiar terraced street
        chimney   by chimney
            I offered a lone blood feather
    to each hearth
        each home

            some pinned these keepsakes
        to their breasts
                                some let them burn
            others buried theirs under peat
        and prayed
for a song thrush to grow

    my mother clutched hers   became Kestrel
            and flew high above the village   she let go
            then circled away
                        quill drifting down
        to the reservoir's
            blue mirror

Peter Wallis

What does it mean?

It does not know its own colours,
cannot name or number its leaves,
and does not know the meaning of *edible*

but it responds to the concepts of *time* and *the seasons*.
It seems to understand sex, but not to anticipate death.
Perhaps, in the sun, in the rain, it experiences pleasure.

More and more often, strolling the allotment
I look at nasturtium's open palms, open mouth, trumpet,

and wonder what it could be trying to shout
or silently gesticulate. But I and it are stuck
in different dreams with incompatible magic.

And there's Hamish digging. He looks up
just enough to give me a nod, though our eyes don't meet.
His wife died only last week.

Mark Pajak

Séance

A candle with its tadpole flame.
The medium asks her questions
and when the dead (eventually)
answer, it's in the same language
spoken by all old houses at night:
an intestinal gurgle in the radiator,
the rats that gallop
through the booming hollow of the loft.

Bollocks, would be my dad's opinion.
Ever the cheeky, straight-talking Glaswegian.
But as for me I can't help but ask,
as I listen to a timber door-frame
softly cluck after the heat of the day,
what is it now, dad, what are you trying to say?

Rosie Garland

Not fallen angel, but in a state of falling

Nazar eye of lapis glass
swinging off the rear view mirror
in a tick tock of luck, (good – bad – good),
a hex of cards and crystal, dragon guarding her throat.
Small strong words like *will* and *no*. Snatching vixen sleep
through afternoons, up at dusk to rip a pomegranate with her teeth.
Wrestles English sky nailed down at all four corners. Throws it off.

Shooting star, yelling to be heard while music blares; first on her feet
for dancing, roaring barefoot up the street, spilling dreams,
hair a ragged flag. Craves nicotine and diesel. Starving
for cities' stew of tongues, stinks, filthy concrete.
She writes a tunnel to the other kingdom,
nails hooked, claws out the shuttered
eye of darkness.

Samatar Elmi

Volcanoes

after Plath

Poems are not afraid of volcanoes
while we ignore signs that warn of *danger*
of *do not cross* and *death*. They draw us in
like a lovers' final embrace; lepidoptera
to the heat of wildfires.

We are the feeble warriors last to be picked
by sergeants of the roll call, we pass
like shadows between frightened soldiers
to make our camp in the Hades
of every no-one's land.

Ours is the magic of eternal spells;
words we pit against the fear of intimacy
against the body's countless deaths,
that we launch against the warnings
and the winds that cannot be stilled.

With ears pressed against the turf
we are first to hear the core rage;
first to stand on the edge of the magma chamber;
the first to burn, to flow as lava,
to settle where the ocean turns to land.

Victoria Gatehouse

The Ivy Crown

Remember   many autumns ago
Dionysus came to squat in the ruined barn

you found him   in the corner of a September dusk
a roosting of bats in his cloak   remember

his berry-dark eyes   warm nectar on his lips
how you swarmed his walls   tender rootlets cast out

remember   how he bound   and unbound you
wove you a slim ivy crown   how you corkscrewed

dead trunks   maenad-wild   wasp-drunk
the tiny acid-green flowers which covered your skin

remember the gloss he laid over your stones   how
the last of the insects came to crawl in your veins

how your leaves turned   from juvenile lobes
to feral hearts   remember how he made you live

how you cut yourself free to live

Gaia Holmes

The Underground Garden

I write to you
from the underground orchards
of Fresno, my back pressed
against the trunk
of an improbable tree
loaded with midnight pears.

This unlikely grove
reminds me of a friend
who grew Arctic lilies
from the lumps of sea-coal
he scrumped from the strand-line
at Skinningrove bay.

If you were here
we'd talk about
all those beautiful girls
trapped in myths and chilly cellars,
trying to breathe light
through worm holes
and hairline cracks.

We'd drink forced rhubarb gin,
eat black bread and pickled lemons
in the geothermal gloom
as we listened to the tiny tick
of waking stones and pips
and watched things sweetening
in the darkness.

In Fresno, California, in the early 1900s Baldassare Forestiere, a Sicilian immigrant crafted a subterranean garden in which he grew vines, orange, lemon and grapefruit trees.

Carola Luther

The Golden Oyster Mushroom Kit

One night a protuberance like a clitoral swelling
pushes into the air, profane, deliciously

> white. It could be an alien being, insolent and sexy
> sticking out a cauliflower tongue, an act

so slow, so obscene who wouldn't want
to watch it happening, this prolapse,

> this tumescence burgeoning in my kitchen? Day two
> and it's widened to a creamy dais, spreads into lip.

Day three it is chalice, and there are more
underneath-buttons demanding caress, to open

> day four to flattening platforms. These like lilies
> tilt upward in a drama of arms, dancers' arms

elegant, exquisite as lace. As the mushrooms grow
so do their power, they are fluid architecture, animal

> almost, almost creatures that have had to keep hidden
> underground, only coming to light in this parallel sphere

where ballerinas perfumed with liquorice pose
in boxes, and dervishes of the loam flare in moon-coloured

> haute couture. Day five and I'm enchanted by innumerable
> pleats in their creams, the milky muumuus, tutus,

fustanellas, the dawn-coloured *traje de flamencos*.
I am entranced by swirl, by swoop of skirt, surgings

        of rippled material, it is flow, it is slow motion
        dance and the oysters are gathering themselves

for some heavenly thing, a transformation – will they leap
become winged, become wings?

                          No. Nothing happens.
        Just a crop of fungi, quiet in the dirt of a kit. Passing

their prime and not even hallucinogenic. Yet
they keep bringing pictures. In the cold

        morning-light of day six I see necks, the fall,
        the arc of necks. Day seven, kings and queens

are pale in a tower, heads tilted to tapestry or prayer
by a pearly window. Day eight it is sunny.

        I follow instructions. The manual
        doesn't warn of fluttering gills of the heart,

the need to say grace. Nor does it name
what later will make me hesitate, hesitate

        to open my mouth and finally accept hot, buttered flesh
        tasting faintly of soil, and fragrant with garlic.

Sarah Westcott

Dowsing

I covet my tree, like lace.
Each leaf a green knife,
clean flower.

A child is inside me
past the long game.
His rotten little trunk broke.

You know his reedy arms root into the earth.

I have a brother, he comes in the drumming
up to water   with a green twitch.

The sky is blue & empty.
At some point in the dream
a long, brief exhalation –

*

I wait, a pear inside,
a robin all over my breasts.

Put your face close now.
My roses are out, in, out,
an apron of flowers.

Feel me, eye of the wood,
living mouth

stuffed with muscle,
so grained & gentle it makes a print,

single flower of lemon & air,
      a small hole,   dogwood;
            a tiny branch that moves ———>

Dorka Tamás

The Witch and the Magician:
Maternal and Paternal Magic in Plath's Writings

In summer 2021, Frieda Hughes put numerous items up for auction at Sotheby's, including her mother's correspondences and personal belongings. The auction was titled, 'Your Own Sylvia: Sylvia Plath's letters to Ted Hughes and other items, property of Frieda Hughes'. The highest-grossing item, which aroused the most public interest and sold for a record £151,200, was Plath's Tarot de Marseille deck. The subsequent discussion around the event highlighted the huge interest from scholars and collectors in Plath's fascination with magic.

In the past, some critics have focused on Plath's perceived connection to the occult, such as Judith Kroll in *Chapters in a Mythology* (1976) and Timothy Materer in 'Sylvia Plath: Occultism as Source and Symptom' published in *Modernist Alchemy* (1995). Feminist critics, such as Sarah Bruton in her dissertation, 'Representations of the Witch in Nineteenth- and Twentieth-Century Women's Writing' (2006), focused on the gender dynamics of poems, like 'Witch Burning' and 'Lady Lazarus' where the poetic persona resembles a witch. Heather Clark, the author of *Red Comet* (2020) also highlighted in her essay, 'Sylvia Plath: an Iconic Life', that when women poets like Plath write about supernatural tropes, they are labelled as playing with "witchcraft, or quasi-occult practices" (3). These examples demonstrate how Plath's work and life are frequently rooted in the vocabulary of the supernatural and emphasise her personal and poetic relationship to magic.

While witches make frequent and obvious appearances in Plath's poetry, she also makes several allusions to the figure of the magus. Plath borrows the imagery of these two opposing supernatural figures from literature, including plays from the early modern witch-hunting period. For Plath, Prospero, the magician from Shakespeare's *The Tempest* represented her paternal relationship. In the play, Prospero's magic is a learnt ability, suggesting the male magician is associated with intellectual powers. This type of magical power is often referred to as "white magic". Sylvia Plath mimics the patriarchal figure of the magician and his powers in her writings, with the father figure often appearing as a dominant and commanding, yet inaccessible, figure. Opposed to the father figure and his learnt magic, maternal figures are frequently associated with witches and their craft. In common speech, witchcraft is used as a synonym for "black magic", which embodies malicious and harmful magic. In contrast to the scholarly white magic, black magic is an innate power, which in literature and culture is associated with women, such as the witches in Shakespeare's *Macbeth*. For Sylvia Plath, the concept of magic falls into these binaries, and in her poetry, she habitually associates "good" magical powers with a paternal male figure and "evil" magic with malicious maternal powers.

Like many of us, Sylvia Plath's relationship to magic began in her childhood. Among the many magical stories and tales Plath read, Grimms' fairy tales were very influential in forming her poetic and creative imagination. Plath's first encounter with the fairy tales was in the original German tales. At Christmas in 1954, her mother gave Plath *Märchen der Brüder Grimm: mit 100 Bildern nach Aquarellen*, printed in 1937 (Steinberg). In the Grimms' fairy tales, magic is primarily associated with maternal figures who are split into the "good", rewarding mother, for example the Fairy Godmother in 'Cinderella', and the "bad", punishing figure of the wicked witch in 'Hansel and Gretel'. In the tales, wicked witches, stepmothers, and sometimes biological mothers who use food for deception, symbolise the opposite of the nurturing mother, suggesting that maternal love is deceitful. The magical powers of witch figures often harm the young heroines: in 'Briar Rose' (also known as 'Sleeping Beauty'), Maleficent curses Aurora, whereas in 'Little Snow White', the evil queen transforms into a peasant woman and poisons Snow White with an apple.

In Plath's poetry, fairy-tale witches and their magical power are symbols of danger or threat: they often suggest transgressive and inadequate motherhood. In the juvenilia poem, 'The Princess and the Goblins', Plath alludes to the fairy tale, 'Briar Rose' when the princess's finger got "stung according to the witch's plan" (CP 333). In another juvenilia, 'Admonitions', Plath evokes the poisonous apple from 'Little Snow White', "The magic golden apples all look good / although the wicked witch has poisoned one" (CP 319). In the lines, the reference to the apple links the biblical symbol with the fairy tale. In 'Admonitions', the witch figure is a symbol of punishment, the outcome of not obeying to rules. These poems reveal Plath's employment of fairy tales, particularly her utilisation of the witch figure as a source of danger. Plath's early poetry is less probing of its subject matter, and she mostly keeps the power dynamics between a young heroine (a princess) and the witch figure symbolising the ambiguous mother figure.

In a somewhat later poem, 'The Disquieting Muses', written in 1957, Plath portrays the mother as a malicious figure who tricks the child with her excessive and ambiguous maternal love. The poem has a nursery rhyme-like rhythm emphasising the child's perspective. 'The Disquieting Muses' starts with an allusion to the curse from 'Briar Rose', "Mother, mother, what illbred aunt / ... Unasked to my christening, that she / Sent these ladies in her stead" (CP 74). Here, the speaker blames the mother for the haunting presence of the headless ladies. In the poem, the uncanny women develop into the figure of witches. Plath also alludes to the gingerbread house of the wicked witch in 'Hansel and Gretel': "Mother, whose witches always, always / Got baked into gingerbread" (CP 75). Here, the mother's baking stands for the contradictions of maternal malevolence and love. Although 'The Disquieting Muses' does not centre on the witch, the weird ladies evoke the uncanny supernatural figures, such as *Macbeth*'s Weird Sisters, whom Plath named as an influence in a radio reading at the BBC. This poem not only shows mature imagery and demonstrates the allusions to the malicious witch figure as a representation of danger, but we can see Plath's awareness of the association between the witch figure's deception with food and her symbolic presence as the "bad mother". Plath's fairy-tale poems often express her ambiguous maternal relationship in which the evil magical powers of the witch symbolise an inescapable maternal presence.

'All the Dead Dears' is another poem from 1957, which portrays maternal hags who haunt the speaker. The poem was inspired by the remains of a woman, mouse, and a shrew kept in the Archaeological Museum in Cambridge, who are watchful witnesses of the living. In 'All the Dead Dears', the descriptive narrative shifts to the psychic life of the speaker, who reimagines the relics as the inescapable maternal presence: "From the mercury-backed glass / Mother, grandmother, greatgrandmother / Reach hag hands to haul me in" (CP 70). The trio of maternal ancestors resembles the three dummies from 'The Disquieting Muses'. Both poems allude to sinister female trios, such as the witches from *Macbeth*. In 'All the Dead Dears', the speaker shifts between calling the spectral figures "dears", "hags", then "darlings", which shows her ambivalent attitude towards the maternal kin. The poem does not portray the maternal ancestors as explicitly evil, yet the speaker's description demonstrates an uneasiness in the relationship. Here, the power of the maternal hags lies in their inescapable presence, which is in parallel to Plath's other poems on witches symbolising maternal malice.

In contrast to the maternal witch figure, the magician frequently appears in Plath's poetry as the dominant but inaccessible father figure. Whereas the influence of *The Tempest* has been highlighted in Plath's poetry, for example, by Ted Hughes in the essay, 'Sylvia Plath and Her Journals' (1982), no one has fully considered Shakespeare's magician figure as an embodiment of Plath's portrayal of her father figure. Like the Grimms' tales, *The Tempest* accompanied Plath in her life and influenced her poetic imagination. In her poetry and private writings, we can see the recurring presence of Shakespeare's play: Plath associated her childhood seascape with the imagery of *The Tempest*, took inspiration from the spirit Ariel in her late poetry, and portrayed the father figure as a larger-than-life, powerful, but inaccessible figure, similar to Prospero. In the play, Prospero primarily uses magic to control nature and others. His magical power comes from scholarly knowledge, which is understood as "good" magic. Yet, his magical control over the island and its creatures make him ambiguous, similar to the maternal witch figures.

Plath's representation of the father and his scholarly knowledge often act as paternal power. The magician controls nature with his magic; likewise, Plath's father-beekeeper uses his intellectual knowledge to dominate the bees. The short story, 'Among the Bumblebees', portrays an idolised domineering father figure and his subsequent death, from the child's perspective. In the story, the father's intellectual power resembles Prospero's use of magic as a form of control. We see the father capturing a bee, which according to Alice, no other father could do: "Then, with a laugh, her father would spread his fingers wide, and the bee would fly out, free, up into the air and away" (JPBL 311). The girl idolises the father's powers; she does not fear his power to control. We can see a parallel between the father's control over the freedom of the bee and Prospero's control and ability to set Ariel free. In Plath's writings, beekeeping is associated with paternal knowledge, which often appears as a tool to control the bees. In the first poem of the sequence, 'The Bee

Meeting', Plath refers to the father as a magus. In the poem, the speaker feels alienated among the beekeepers, and she calls on the father for help: "I am the magician's girl who does not flinch" (CP 212). Her self-identification with the Miranda-like daughter figure suggests that beekeeping is associated with the father's intellectual knowledge. The speaker is not suitable for beekeeping; therefore, she cannot continue her father's legacy. In 'The Arrival of the Bee Box', the speaker further contemplates her relationship to the bees. Lynda K. Bundtzen notes that in the poem, the speaker's decision between control or granting freedom to the bees compares to Prospero's decision to free Ariel, the spirit (167). The poetic persona's uneasy relationship with the bees expresses ambiguity with the paternal knowledge of beekeeping used to control the bees. We see traces of Prospero later in 'Daddy', in which Plath more violently rejects the domineering patriarchal father figure.

In Plath's other poems, for example, 'Full Fathom Five' and 'On the Decline of Oracles', the father is a larger-than-life figure who emerges from the imagery of *The Tempest*. The speaker longs for the paternal connection, which resembles the relationship between the beekeeper and her daughter. At the same time, she also fears him, and his presence signals danger. In these poems, *The Tempest* functions as background material for the lost paternal relationship, which is recovered from the sea imagery. The poem 'Full Fathom Five' borrows its title from Ariel's song from the play on the mourning of Ferdinand's father. Here, Plath's portrayal of the father is god-like: he has "white hair, white beard"; he is "The old myth of origins", yet "Unimaginable" (CP 92). The father is a dangerous and dominant figure, whom the speaker both fears and desires, yet she cannot locate him in her imagination. In 'Full Fathom Five', *The Tempest* functions as a literary and littoral medium, through which the image of the father figure is accessed. The speaker evokes the seascape associated with the play to recreate the paternal relationship. Plath's poems influenced by the imagery of *The Tempest* are often preoccupied with the paternal absence. There is perceived tension in his figure being both inaccessible and paradoxically inescapable. He likewise reappears in 'Daddy', where the father is the "head in the freakish Atlantic" (CP 222).

For Plath, magic is an important source of poetic inspiration, which signals the ambiguities of her maternal and paternal relationships. In contrast to the proto-feminist 'Lady Lazarus', several of Plath's witch figures are associated with the maternal presence. By comparing the ambiguous mother figure to wicked witches, Plath expresses the inadequacy of maternal love, which is both insufficient and excessive. While the portrayal of witches is explicit in Plath's writings, she only alludes to the magus figure. For Plath, the male magical power is intellectually desirable, yet deeply rooted in patriarchy, and is also a form of control. The father figure and his powers are equally desired and feared by Plath's speakers, which represent the ambiguities of the paternal bond. Plath's representation of her parental relationships can be read as her differentiating between female and male magical powers. The witch and the magician are the two most well-known supernatural figures in Western culture. Their figures are present from early modern literature and across fairy tales, which prompted Plath to consider magic as a gendered power. Like many of us, Plath was influenced by her encounters with literary magic, which accompanied her throughout her life.

Works Cited:

Bundtzen, Lynda K. *The Other Ariel*. Stroud : Sutton Publishing, 2005.

Clark, Heather. 'Sylvia Plath: An Iconic Life', *Women's History Review* (2021): 1-14. 2021.

Crowther, Gail and Peter K. Steinberg. *These Ghostly Archives: The Unearthing of Sylvia Plath*. US; UK: Fonthill Media, 2017.

Plath, Sylvia. *Johnny Panic and the Bible of Dreams*. New York: Buccaneer Books, 1979.

The Collected Poems. Ed. Ted Hughes. New York: HarperCollins, 2008.

Steinberg, Peter K. *Library of Sylvia Plath*. n.d. 13 Dec. 2021. <https://www.librarything.com/catalog/SylviaPlathLibrary/yourlibrary>.

MOTHERS & FATHERS

Moniza Alvi

The Weighing

She tells me how, when I wasn't feeding well
she'd take me down the lane to her neighbour
the other English woman, an inspector of schools.
My mother would stand on this lady's scales
with – and then without me.
So that was how I was weighed

at that difficult time in Pakistan.
1954. The sky was burning blue.
It was later, a few years later, that I started
as they say, to thrive.
Am I thriving now? I ask myself.
What do I weigh in my flesh and bones –

in the secret inside the scales?
The difference then between my mother
with and without me – was it infinitesimal?
Now she glances at me as if in wonderment
as I sit in the armchair opposite
and Norfolk light floods the care home windows.

By a sleight of hand her story
becomes my own.
I pass it on here – a little of it.

Mari Ellis Dunning

A Sudden Mother (Staying on the postnatal ward during Covid-19)

There is no sleep here, where women shuffle, barefoot.
Elasticated waistbands. Nightgowns trailing linoleum.
We are pale and bloodless ghosts. We are waning
moons. We do not speak to one another. In a bed
feet from mine, someone chokes, a sob thick as toffee
cloying her throat. An indifferent curtain hangs between us.
Somewhere on the ward, a baby cries, pitching its vowels
to the ceiling fan. The baby isn't mine. My baby is a lost
creature, hibernating in a sterile incubator, a corridor stretching
between us like a deep lake. Tubes like terrible worms
curling his nostrils. Burrowing into his hands. He has shaken
something loose in me, like coins rattling in an old tin. I swell
and I leak. A sudden mother. For a week, it goes like this:
me, wringing my hands at his cribside, my stupid pupils dry
and wide. Watching his heartbeat form steady mountaintops
against the darkness. Friends framed like portraits,
stuttering their congratulations through phone screens.
His father, pitched miles away, butting at doors that scream:
                              Stop.
                                  No entry.

Penelope Shuttle

mother as wet nurse

when at midnight
or at dawn
we spoke
the unsaid language
of the breast
an ordinary room
gave us blessing
glanced at us
in wonder
you and I

those times
long past the owl's bedtime
or before the bee
began his day's work
I've kept safe
through
mixed-blessing years
assured at least
when all is lost
of the remembered infant
in my arms
how our hushed idiom
was richest utterance

Martin Kratz

What I didn't say / Was ich nicht gesagt habe

I used to catch languages hiding in other languages.
I was wrong to think of a language as a kind
of animal shaking in the heather.
Some just give themselves away – like waves
trying to relate to you the shape of their ground.
Others – tunnelling – leave molehills soft as fontanelles,
making pockets in language to fill.
No one dies without some apology outstanding.

　　When a clam shuts,
it's propelled forward on a jet of water in water.
My language was always more like that:
it (ach)e(d u)nspoken through the other.
Asked: *am I the sunshine with a moon's accent or?*
It should've been so easy to say: *come out, new light.*

Sharon Black

Departures

                    – a tail that won't stop
chasing itself: Dad has
parked the car, lifted out my luggage,
we're heading towards Departures,
his sideways stoop, clipped steps
propelling us ahead, Mum clutching
her coat collar, me between them
wheeling my two blue cases, the yellow sign
above the automatic doors shining
like a soon-to-be-forgotten thought,
                                just there –
an off-hand remark as the flight times
lurch into view, all the longing and
effusiveness he rushes through, something about
how it always pays to leave enough time.

Roy McFarlane

After hearing of Plath likening despair to an owl sitting on her chest, I find you in Fuseli's *The Nightmare*

The woman in deep sleep.
Almost hovering above her bed
body stretched, draped, arched,
a creature sits on her abdomen
abdodere, the place of hiding.

This is where I find you, hiding deep
talons clenching a constricting heart
my heart desires to know you, daddy.

Are you the sire that haunts me?
Dark and headless in the background
the young man inside cries to know you, daddy.

Are you the despair, the fire and fury?
A volcano that erupts without notice,
the anger that boils within to know you, daddy

don't you realise you're supposed to be
my legacy, my jazz funk, my spirituals,
my way into my history, my testimony,
my beginning and my ending,
the weight to know you, daddy.

Julie Irigaray

Women of Aquitaine

My mother knew I wasn't meant to be a princess:
I was more of the Robin Hood type, fighting with
fists and kicks for the outcasts – until I almost got
expelled from school. My only doll suffered the same
fate as Marie-Antoinette and ended up flushed down
the toilet. At birthday parties I sneaked into my male
friends' bedrooms to try on their King Arthur costumes.

So for my first holiday, my mother brought me
to fortified castles instead of Disneyland Paris.
She drove east for five hours to reach
places of persecution and teach me
tolerance through the story of the Cathars.
She bought me an Occitan cross
as a talisman and told me everything about

the Plantagenet queen from our region
who enthralled men and fought in the crusades.
My mother passed on her love for history
via blood transfusion. When I wanted to
become a palaeontologist, she never dismissed
it as a childish dream, unlike my father.
We roamed across the south-west of France

to visit prehistoric spots from the Lascaux
caves to dinosaur sites where she watched me
excavating fake fossils with other children.
Because my mother knew I wasn't meant to be
a princess, but a knight, a scientist,
more than a queen, a poet maybe –
something not expected of me.

Paul Stephenson

Show Homes

My mother longed for skirting boards
and coving throughout, the occasional dado rail,
wanted everything modern, everything finished.

It would be perfect. A lounge in Magnolia,
a fitted kitchen in Mimosa,
a downstairs loo in Apple Green.

The Kingston. The Richmond. The Excelsior.
She wanted the one all done out
that doubled up as their showroom-cum-office.

She'd waste their time. Every time.
She was in no position to buy.

She'd give them her details,
take their brochures, pages of gloss.
She'd dream of upstairs, all that hanging space.

Niamh Prior

Artefacts

I curate an assemblage of your things:
your thesis dated November 1953
'A New Route to Isoquinolines',
carefully typed and carbon copied,
letters blurring like an old tattoo.
Another fatter one dated autumn 1956,
navy hardback with a gold embossed title,
'Studies in N-Methylamides',
typed on a writer with a wonky 'a'.
Hexagrams drawn by hand, in hair-thin
strokes, cluster like honeycomb cells.
In the photo it's London in 1958.
Curved cars and double-deckers
blur by behind you in black and white.
You look like JFK in your trench-coat,
newspaper tucked under your left arm,
pipe in the right corner of your mouth,
your hair slicked up in a cresting wave.
I know what year your Parker fountain
pen was made, but not who gave it to you.
Were you diligent with those theses
or did you rush them right to the deadline?
What do I have that is real? A memory
like a faded film flickering, in which
you pick me up in the front garden –
I am wearing my lemon-yellow jumper
with a basket of flowers embroidered
over my heart. You swing me around
and around in the sunshine. I have
nothing new to say about love
or loss or death. I gather your things
like an animal, on instinct, a crow
dropping twigs into a chimney,
expecting they will eventually pile up
and form somewhere solid to rest.

Jennifer Lee Tsai

Risk

Dostoyevsky sold his second wife Anna's possessions
to fund his gambling addiction.
She was a stenographer.
In a letter to his first wife's sister,
he claimed that the secret of success
in gambling was *terribly silly and simple.*
It is important to keep *under constant control*
and avoid *getting excited, no matter how the game shifts.*
In his novella, *The Gambler,* the narrator asks
'*For why is gambling a whit worse than any other method*
of acquiring money? How, for instance, is it worse than trade?'

In the early years of their marriage, my father sold
my mother's 22 carat gold jewellery
to pay off his gambling debts.
The pursuit of a dream. Triple eights.
My mother's tears fell. But what's mine is yours.
The traditional Chinese character for love, 愛,
contains a heart in its centre – 心 –
but in the 1950s, the Communist Party simplified
the written script to encourage literacy.
The character for love lost its heart 爱.
This did not affect my parents.

During the 1970s, in Liverpool
when my father asked my grandfather's permission
to marry my mother, my grandfather asked
for a larger dowry than was expected at the time.
When Dostoyevsky first fell in love
with a woman named Maria, he sent her
his last roubles and a proposal of marriage.
He told the coachman to wait for her answer
before making the week-long journey
back through the snow.

In *Crime and Punishment,* he tells us
that facts aren't everything.
Knowing how to deal with the facts
is at least half the battle.
It is often thrilling to walk a tightrope.
To feel your heart beating fast.
I would like to gamble but I'm afraid.
I've lost too many times before.
I am my father's daughter.

Tiffany Atkinson

Small flame for Sylvia

I put two candles in my handbag
and drive to North Tawton
where my parents lived for three years
in the un-tuned radio of early marriage.
That was still the sixties.
You'd have been a faint horizon of white static.
I'm not sure my mother ever read a poem.
Even I stare flatly back at them occasionally thinking wtf.
Can a town be built entirely out of milk and hasty marriages?
You weren't any stamp of feminist and nor was mum.
You cooked and stitched. You managed house.
You joined the WI. My god.
Sashaying down the high street with a plate of nippled cakes.
The crackling american corsage of you.
What can you do by an english country churchyard
with two infants and a titan-slaying talent in the sixties.
Cry into the onions like my mother.
Coax the sweetness out of motherhood small spoon by small spoon.
Show your children how to put things softly in the ground.
Climb to the top of the house at night
and drive the spur of your perfectionism
hard into the slippy flank of language.
What a comet's tail of ash and gold stars!
Still the dairy lorries swing their huge fumes through the square.
Prams bounce past with little parasols.
The yew tree is the one dark point. I'll light them there.
Another woman with a city haircut shakes the shadows
from herself and stands to leave. You're
a wedge in the chest of every poet-girl who ever knelt
in Blackwells on a dreary half-term afternoon.
The tree was split and nobody could get you back in.
I put you quietly in my schoolbag. Always
it's like opening a secret. Cool and lunar like an old
refrigerator raided in the night. Watch us stand there
all your sweet besotted daughters in old t-shirts thinking what now.

Degna Stone

Lines That Jar

This article quotes racist language and other phrases that readers may find offensive.

Isn't it something to fall in love with a poem? When a poem communicates an exact feeling at exactly the right time in your life, it can open up a way of understanding yourself a little more. So many people feel that way about Sylvia Plath, whether they came to her as teenagers, in early adulthood or later in life as I did. I'd known about Plath since my teenage years (she was a perennial favourite amongst the willowy, angst-ridden girls in the sixth-form common room) but I'd never really read her work until collecting *The Guardian*'s *Great Poets of the 20ᵗʰ Century* series. By this time I was a young(ish) mother to two small children and 'You're', the first poem in this curated selection, presented gorgeously weird observations that resonated with my own rebirth into the surreal and exhausting world of parenthood. Plath's mastery over simile and metaphor surprised and delighted me.

The Guardian's bitesize edition of Plath poems must also have been my introduction to the racist language that creeps into her work, but I somehow managed to skip over it, or make allowances for it. I wanted to lean into the world of this remarkable poet whose influence extends beyond her short lifetime, so I put the troubling phrases down to being symptomatic of their time (which doesn't really cut it as an excuse when you consider that the American civil rights movement was in full swing by the time Plath died in 1963).

Over the years, even as I marvelled at Plath's use of imagery and her defiant brand of feminism in poems like 'The Applicant', the not-infrequent occurrences of offensive terminology in her work held me at a distance. In the poem 'Daddy', which appears in her posthumous collection *Ariel*, she employs a phrase to describe a Polish person considered to be an ethnic slur (then and now), and her references to Jews and Jewishness are also unsettling. There is something inherently disturbing about Plath's evocation of the Holocaust, a borrowing of an identity of the oppressed and persecuted that is shocking. Deliberately so? I wasn't so sure, but Plath's appropriation of Jewish suffering as a metaphor for her own mental anguish in itself is seen by some Plath scholars as an act of anti-Semitism.

The racist language in the collection's title poem 'Ariel' is more direct. The introduction of the n-word in the fourth stanza takes me by surprise on every re-reading. There is a violence and painfulness to its inclusion.

> Nigger-eye
> Berries
> Cast dark
> Hooks

Who's to say whether this use of racist language is an indicator of racism in the poet? Using the n-word as adjective rather than racial slur was apparently not uncommon during Plath's lifetime. Even in the 1990s a minority of people didn't understand that the n-word, in and of itself, was offensive. When I was re-sitting my A levels, a mature student couldn't understand why the Black and Asian students in the class were offended when he insisted that the n-word was just a description of a colour "like *n......-brown* shoe polish". I guess he would have been from the same generation as Plath, a year or two older or younger perhaps.

As a Black person, it is impossible for me to divorce the n-word from its racist origins. And the fact that the term was used to describe a particular colour simply adds insult to injury. Casual, unintended racism is still racism. So what does the reader do? Skip over the offensive lines, pretend they don't exist, or acknowledge that the inclusion of racist words or phrases says something about the poet as well as the times she existed in?

Plath's poem 'Thalidomide', which uses language that would be considered racist and ableist now, could be read as a product of its times:

> Half-brain, luminosity –
> Negro, masked like a white,
> Your dark
> Amputations crawl and appall –

The word "negro" was still in frequent use in the '50s and '60s and society's everyday discrimination against disabled people was prevalent. In this exploration of disability (specifically that caused when the drug thalidomide was taken during the early stages of pregnancy), Plath's imagery conjures up something to be feared and pitied, whilst maintaining an ambiguity as to whether she feels empathy or horror for "the thing I am given". The "product of its time" defence might acquit the writer, but we are not reading Plath in the past, and to continue to ignore offensive tropes within her work seems like a wilful act of erasure.

Elsewhere, Plath uses the well-worn conventions of associating white with purity and black with oblivion, depression and destruction. Darkness and blackness in their literal sense as an absence of light: "Morning has been blackening, // […] / starless and fathomless, a dark water" ('Sheep in Fog'). Darkness, in essence, is something that has the power to frighten. Something to be feared. Something to ward off if possible. "Black equals evil", "white equals good" is an easy shorthand that we all recognise but in Plath's work even that dichotomy isn't quite so straightforward. Whiteness doesn't always represent light and peacefulness, and the racism that appears in Plath's work is not a black and white issue.

In addition to the unambiguously racist language that crops up, there is also a seeming fear of Black people in Plath's work. The striking discomfort and anxiety expressed in 'The Arrival of the Bee Box' has an unsettling effect: "With the swarmy feeling of African hands / Minute and shrunk for export, / Black on black, angrily clambering". It is not the use of the phrase "black on black" (though it brings to mind the racist trope of "black on black crime" when read through a modern lens) but the "swarmy feeling" and "angrily clambering" that troubles me. An othering that is hard to articulate, the potential danger of a swarm of bees conflated with the potential danger of enslaved Africans. The latent violence of imprisoned captives plays into the stereotype of Black men as "savage brutes" who pose a mortal danger to white women. This is a trope that gained traction with the white supremacist film *The Birth of a Nation* in 1915 and filtered into the general consciousness. Plath's hive exposes the fear that consumes those in positions of power, a fear that leads to a continuation of the status quo rather than freeing those held captive. Reflecting on the speaker's power over the bees, the poem ends, "The box is only temporary". Maybe here Plath recognises and acknowledges the harm caused by white supremacist power structures and the role of white women within them.

Stumbling across racist language in a literary text creates a violence. It's a figurative violence which nonetheless has a physical impact. It hurts. Racism hurts. Even the kind of racism that can be easily ignored or dismissed if your skin colour has never caused you to be racialised. For such readers it might be possible then to miss the subtle (and not so subtle) moments of othering or exclusion that occur in the work of the writers we revere. But when those moments are pointed out it is no longer a question of the work "being of its time", the act of reading brings the work into "our time".

In her novel *The Bell Jar*, which has been described as a satirical novel, Plath observes the mores and conventions of mid-twentieth-century American life through her protagonist Esther Greenwood (widely regarded as a proxy for Plath herself). Its primary focus is on sexual politics and gender, told through the lens of mental illness caused by the unreasonable stifling of a person's soul because they happen to be born female. This was a time when Dior's New Look was sweeping across post-war Europe and America. The tiny, cinched waists and voluminous skirts created an idealised and idolised female silhouette. Impossible to achieve without vast amounts of underpinning. Even as this look gave way to a (slightly) more natural silhouette in the 1960s, the ideal was still hyper feminine and impractical. Women as objects. Through this exploration of the superficial world of fashion *The Bell Jar* also reveals the stark absence of "otherness" in accepted forms of beauty.

The racism in *The Bell Jar* is, paradoxically, more obvious and less pervasive than I remember on first reading the novel in my thirties. People who aren't white (especially other women) are largely absent from the narrative and whilst there are only a dozen or so specific incidences of racism that stood out, they are undeniably there.

Is Plath's portrayal of Esther a critique of the world that she grew up in or does it betray her own racism? Like using the n-word to describe a colour, the invidious American idiom "free, white, and twenty-one", which Plath's character Buddy Willard uses in *The Bell Jar*, could be seen as another signifier of racism in her work. Today, using racist language without critique is a pretty firm indicator of racist beliefs but in the mid-twentieth century it was normalised to denigrate, belittle and dismiss the feelings of people of colour in everyday language.

It's a struggle to read *The Bell Jar* and ignore those jarring moments where racial otherness is depicted as being rooted in ugliness or weirdness. Esther's self-loathing is seen in descriptions of herself: "I looked yellow as a Chinaman. Ordinarily I would have been nervous about my dress and my odd colour"; "I noticed a big, smudgy-eyed Chinese woman staring idiotically into my face. It was only me, of course. I was appalled to see how wrinkled and used-up I looked"; "The face in the mirror looked like a sick Indian". Esther's self-disgust is palpable but it's not only herself that she describes in crude racist language. Plath uses racial signifiers as shorthand for the objectionable, for example, when Doreen, Esther's sort-of best friend, doesn't flinch when touched on her bare arm by a man she's just met, she is described as being "dusky as a bleached blonde negress". Elsewhere Esther describes Peruvians as being "ugly as Aztecs" and recounts a would-be boyfriend's description of a white sex worker as having "suspiciously thick lips and rat coloured skin". Plath rarely uses racial imagery in a positive light and crudely stereotypes Eastern Europeans and Mediterraneans too, reflecting the mistrust of even those groups who began to be more readily accepted as part of the "white" hierarchy following the Second World War.

Using the term "negro" to describe a Black person was still considered a polite convention in America at the time *The Bell Jar* was written but the unquestionably racist depiction of the Black hospital lunch assistant as an eye-rolling fool was a choice the author made. Was Plath critiquing, and deliberately arguing against, the dominance of entitled, WASP (white, Anglo-Saxon, protestant) culture in America? Or was she simply a part of it? Is Plath's use of racist language in her writing "of its time" or is it plain old racism?

On its own *The Bell Jar* doesn't indicate racism in the heart or mind of Sylvia Plath. Esther Greenwood is probably racist, in the way that any middle-class, white person growing up in an America still segregated by Jim Crow laws might be. Society on both sides of the Atlantic was unquestioningly geared toward white dominance, and white supremacist ideology (as we understand the term today) was largely unchallenged by those who benefited from it.

Looking through Plath's journals it's possible to infer that she wasn't completely unaware of racial injustice in the world. On 10 May 1958, she refers to a fundraising drive for scholarships for African students in apartheid-era South Africa "which my conscience has been nagging me to contribute to". Later, in between talk of war and the Miss America beauty pageant, she refers to the harsh sentence meted out to a Black person convicted of theft:

> War is talked of again – Chinese communists, fareast-news breaks in grimly. Moonshot rivalry. Death sentence of negro stealing $1.95. How? Hatred, madness, bigotry. One cannot retreat.   (Sept 5, 1958. pg. 419)

This shows compassion surely and could be seen as evidence that Plath wasn't inherently racist, but the journals also reveal a casual use of anti-Semitic and racist tropes:

> She came bounding up in a suede jacket with glasses, a long Jewy nose and open grin, and fresh crimped high-fronted hairdo (done in Winkleigh that morning).
>   (March 2, 1962. pg. 636)

> Pictures of the three daughters in wedding dress - - - an album of the model daughter: hard-faced, black hair, a Jewy rapaciousness.   (July 4, 1962. pg.664)

> So we talked about little things, how words lose their meaning when you repeat them over and over; how all people of the Negro race look alike until you get to know them individually...   (Extract 11, 1950. pg. 14)

There is a throwaway air to these excerpts, and although the language used is offensive and insensitive it could be argued that it is ignorance rather than malice behind them.

The "product of her time" defence keeps returning but the 1950s and '60s were a time when people where actively fighting against systemic racism and prejudice. Pointing out the racist language within Plath's writing is not a call to retrofit modern sensibilities onto the work of a long-dead writer, but in the sixty years since Plath's death the world has changed and will keep changing. Modern readers will approach her work with all the baggage of the intervening years; future readers will bring some new stuff that we can't possibly imagine from this vantage point in time. We can't know for sure if Plath the person was or wasn't racist (by the standards of her own times); we can only interpret what is left behind in her poetry and prose. What we can do is remain in conversation with that work and consider what her writing tells us about our own time and how things have (or haven't) changed.

Confronting the racism within Plath's work means confronting racism within society and within ourselves. A refusal to acknowledge or challenge it allows hatred and fear to perpetuate. To allow racist language in our favourite texts to go unchallenged is an acceptance of racism. We can't learn if we don't interrogate and converse with the past. This isn't a call to abandon Plath – for many readers she will have been there for them at a time when they felt alone and misunderstood.

No one has to abandon their literary heroes. The way I read Plath now is a bit like my still being a die-hard fan of The Smiths. Morrissey might want to exclude me from his "England for the English", but The Smiths were a fundamental part of my adolescence. I can understand why other former fans can no longer comfortably listen to their songs, but I won't give them up.

I choose to dip in and out of Plath's poetry, avoiding the poems that exclude me (deliberately or inadvertently) and enjoying the poems that give me hope, make me smile or remind me that poetry can rescue you from despair just in the nick of time. In 'Mushrooms', a poem for the meek, the quiet, the multitudes, Plath may not have been writing to, or for, anyone outside her own lived experience but it still speaks to me:

> Perfectly voiceless,
> Widen the crannies,
> Shoulder through holes. […]
>
> We shall by morning
> Inherit the earth.
> Our foot's in the door.

A poem is for everyone, anyone. The overlooked and underestimated can still find solace and comfort in Plath's poetry, you just need to know which poems to avoid.

Works Cited

Plath, S. 1960. *The Colossus and Other Poems*. London. Heinemann

Plath, S. 1963. *The Bell Jar*. London. Faber and Faber

Plath, S. 1965. *Ariel*. London. Faber and Faber

Plath, S. 1971. *Winter Trees*. London. Faber and Faber

Plath, S. and Drabble, M., 2008. *Great Poets of the 20th Century: Sylvia Plath*. London. Guardian.

Plath, S. and Kukil, K., 2014. *The Journals of Sylvia Plath 1950-1962*. London. Faber and Faber.

Poems Referenced

From *The Colossus and Other Poems:* 'Mushrooms'

From *Ariel:* 'Sheep in Fog', 'The Applicant', 'Ariel', 'Daddy', 'You're', 'The Arrival of the Bee Box'

From *Winter Trees:* 'Thalidomide'

NATURE

Anastasia Taylor-Lind

Welcome to Donetsk

You teach me this wartime trick –
to look for living pot plants
in the windows on Kievska Avenue.
Most are crisped and brown.

But one green geranium
and a succulent spider plant
offer proof of life
for the person who waters them.

Whole apartment blocks are abandoned.
Collapsed telephone lines,
blown-up branches
litter the road.

No voices,
no tinkering metalwork in the distance,
no buses, no playing children.
Leaves rustle white noise.

You say *It's like Sunday, every day*.
Stray dogs and swallows,
and the soft thud of shelling.

Caleb Parkin

Ricinus in Spring, 2020

a golden shovel after 'Poppies in July'

Hot, silent April. You sit at a little
Formica table, enquire about this bloody
egg cup, full of reddish water. He skirts
the issue, says it's just a seed, resting there
to soak, preparing for the ground. *There are*
poisons everywhere, he whispers. *Fumes*
in airducts which life has colonised, nature that
flourishes in death. He sips oolong, goes on, *I*
will plant it at the edge of the bed, but you cannot
mistake it for food, cannot smoke it or touch
its spiky leaves. Now you can't recall where
Ricinus has rooted, in which spot its toxins are
concealed. His grubby palms gesture to your
garden. And you imagine all the opiates
erupting from Afghan fields, the pollens in your
nostrils, the masses in cities' tubes. Nauseous,
you open a cupboard, swollen with capsules.

Colin Bancroft

Raspberry Picking at High Force

It is too late in the season now.
Along the woodland verge the greens brown.
The bushes are bare but for a few
Shrivelled chandeliers, tiny blood clots
On the canes' dark veins. The falls drop.
The river mills, churning the dark slurry
Of a dead year. The trees have begun
To seep. Bracken rots in the understorey.
But give it time and the colour will come back,
The raspberries will grow sweet and fat
In these thickets like the tongues
Of a choir. The birds will sing again,
Transfusing summer into their songs.
Do not worry. It will not be long.

Zaffar Kunial

Tulips

nothing to do with two lips
one of the other things

the Persian-speaking turbaned
Rumi was said to have said

was that the cleverest thing
was not to be clever

the one tulip these two eyes stare at is
near home, up the hill, on Plath's grave

a doubly real thing, and nothing
to do with pupils

Nina Mingya Powles

Parliament Hill Fields

November 2021

I move through softened oak and clover
where you walked. Pink tendrils surface.
The last time I visited you on the hill
above the valley, there was a jar:
six ball-point pens, a key, two tulip husks
like dried hearts. I make note of objects

left behind. When sunlight cuts this way
through bright cold, how far am I from the lake
that day with my parents when I was thirteen,
when I held my palm against the ice?
Floating around us, each broken piece of glacier
was its own small valley of blue light.

How far am I, here? I can make out
my garden over on the other side where
one day a friend, studying my birth chart,
said I'd always be home close to a shoreline.
What shape this shore might take, she couldn't say.
The evening sound of parakeets and
passing trains drowned out our words.
She knew my love's obsessed with buried rivers.
He always knows when one is near.
Even the deepest ones will not forget
these sensations at the surface:
the blue of distance, of snowmelt.
The language of a field in late autumn:
saplings, wingbeats, birdshadow,
cypresses reeling from the speed
of each train. In the earth
I feel them coming one by one.

Daniel Fraser

Rot, rot, rot

confronting a picture by Emil Nolde

I.
You can watch the year burn as it heals, letting flames
scatter on the flat ground. Take these
cooled suns that nod on the fields in blue-dark,
staining the long blades of shadow and corn.

Poppies sprung from the cold mud, a symbol
you know why given, what for. Solemn flares
set to scald across the common,
white roots sinking to make the lid for graves.

II.
Scruffy foam, dandyish and flushed; the faint twitch
of memories in conflict. They dance, rasp,
beat mimicking the spool and plunge of stars.

Lice forage there, iron beads, plate-casings
adrift in the soft tilth. Soil unworked by salvage,
the wet blood of labour, nature's reclamation.

III.
Blank cries recoil from the scrub, heads
lopped, an unseemly frill. Too easily they shake

out beauty, colour, seed; their costly oaths
rendering our pain: diffuse, resounding.

Sarah Wimbush

Little Red

In this strange heat
they motor across window-frame continents,
oceans of glass, red-brick deserts.
Busy going nowhere.
The smallest are barely here: grains
of strawberry Space Dust, spinning gems.
Occasionally, the pin-head Pac-Men collide,
or dance, just like we do in the street:
hesitate, apologise, then re-route.
How miniscule their minds must be, their hearts.
When I pick up *The Time Machine* by H. G. Wells
I notice one has climbed aboard.
Braille feet sample letters,
pausing at times to digest a word.
I try to blow the spiderling away
but Little Red holds on to the end
of a sentence – its Super Mite legs
barely visible. Brushed aside
it is forever blood across the page.

David Borrott

On the verge

Here, where the river dumps its mud and the tide
folds back over the foreshore, diminishing,
we slip through the dunes, emerge to the wind
broadcasting nonsense across the expanse,
racing like the afternoon light towards that gap between clouds
where the day is determined to end.

After the stubby beach, a succession of ripples,
a stratum leased from the ocean, a wet dais
of indecipherable hieroglyphs which our boots scuff,
then on through channels of brine,
past exercising horses and a dog barking at seagulls
chasing them despite their wings, their easy lifts
out of its element.

Salt dries in the sand clefts, whelks
empty into themselves, bivalves lie halved
and a glut of razor shells tally what is lost.
The sea far off is no chorus line lifting its skirts,
only a thin white chain turning as it is pulled.
A dangerous thing that we can't seem to close on.

Behind, the spikes of the town retract, and it's just us
and our findings; wireweed, an erratic rock,
a third of a fish, on this undulating plateau
with lugworms millioning the mud,
with a sky that can't wait. The wind
has our ears, we seem elsewhere,
not just on this wet and dry plinth

under daylight sliding away
and the night charging. If that trope
of mind as a landscape is valid, then I know this place.
I have been here often on that ledge
between sleeping and wakefulness, where opposites conjoin,
where imagination beachcombs and the deep seeps in.

Jean Sprackland

Snigs

Lake with its hair brushed sleek,
lake a brown arm laid on a tabletop,
or a tray of glass pieces, shaken and shaken –
I'd like to praise its truthfulness,
but it distracts and deflects,
it shuts up its secrets.
Glass eels have been shucked from its waters.
Barely there, like newlyweds,
one a long thin window for the other.
Compass needles balanced in murk.
Migrants from far upriver, youngsters
making the eelfare, as their forebears did,
but in run-off, microplastics, hormone disruptors.
Then there's legend of yellow eels.
Swam on dry land, over chert and rough grass
to get here. It was night, no one saw them.
I have seen them salted and coiled
in a tall jar on a museum shelf,
but here they are an article of faith.
Creatures not of habit but vocation.
Each a chink of moon, at lurk in the sump.
I claim them as kin: not roach or bream,
slung in refracted warmth, and rising for flies;
but snigs, slunk in the dark,
hunting its inroads, sucking meat from bone.
Fishsnake, mudribbon, wyrm,
unword me now,
let me come to the edge and slip under.
I want that still fire, quartered in shadow.
I want the long years of silvering,
and the slow growth of an idea –
the one idea that matters.

Bhanu Kapil

Poem for the last day

Today and yesterday: abundant red flowers. Parked my car, then turned. Tulip, a bizarre offering. I wanted to place that flower, at the last moment, on the step. The threshold. A foot. But did not.

On my last day at the university, I am thinking of the students of colour, the staff members of colour, the faculty of colour, and the non-contracted workers of colour. The desire to make an offering is for them: then, now, not yet. Too red: tulip + snow.

I see you. On the last day, we say things like this. To stop the day. To ask: What the exact right. Next thing. Could be. Plants, warmth, tents, signs, strangers, and water are ecologies present even here. You're constantly slowing it down, the university, to see what's there.

A trace.

In the break between classes, I walk to the green. The administrative hall, surrounded by landscaping materials intended to evoke the sea, is dark. Lights off. Bright yellow dots behind my eyes, azure dots of the rain on the glass of the hall itself. That's it then. Here are some images from the protest aftermath: a wetness and darkness where the dirt was.

And there is the red tulip. In the darkness beneath the tree, it splits the icy air in two.

Broken-hearted, I put my head down, right there on the mud.

Nobody saw. Was I there?

Drove home.

Lowered myself into the hot salt bath.

Nina Billard Sarmadi

The Crow

I once saw a crow.
It froze into the night like the rough strings of a tapestry,
And I saw its eyes, two new moons, painted with stars.
It ran from tree to tree, jaggedly, like a highwayman fleeing on his horse.

I once saw a crow in plain daylight.
It was clawing soft, damp turf.
It was stout and black, with a long strong beak.
It could have been the shadow of a kingfisher,
Or the kingfisher its shadow on another world.

I once heard a crow on a January night.
Its cries echoed in the air,
Like two pieces of tarnishing silver, rubbing together,
Rolling over the valleys of thick, dark night.

Devina Shah

Symbol, Canvas and Portal:
Nature in the Plathian Universe

The natural world suffuses Sylvia Plath's poetic universe. Intricately woven through her body of work, it functions in diverse ways. Across *The Colossus, Crossing the Water,* and *Ariel,* landscapes, animals, and plants feature, at times as subjects of the poems, at times as springboards for the discovery of internal environments, and at times as portals for the speaker's journey beyond the boundaries of the poem.

In bringing Plath's exploration and expression of nature into a 21st century critical context, it is tempting to seek out an eco-poetical reading, that is, to see if she can be reimagined for the Anthropocene era as an environmentalist. The closest Plath comes to providing us with this type of "ecological message poetry" is perhaps in her Bee poems, which close *Ariel,* and in her walking poems, which feature in *Crossing the Water.* Both selections vividly dramatise ecopoetics as an interaction between organism and its environment.

Plath as nature poet is a descendent of Anglo and German Romanticism, exhibited obviously in some of her earlier poetry where animals and landscapes, particularly creatures from the agricultural world, are subject matter in their own right and objects of awe, wonder, and contemplation. This is evident in *The Colossus,* in poems such as 'Sow' and 'The Eye-Mote', where her work is closer to classic nature poetry. This first collection also uses nature imagery in the conventional poetic way, that is it expresses flowers, plants, trees, birds and bees, among other elements, as symbols.

By the time we arrive at *Ariel,* a shift has taken place. As Frieda Hughes mentions in the introduction to the restored edition of her mother's fame-making collection, the poems that were written towards the end of 1961 "had an urgency, freedom, and force that was quite new in her work". Hughes describes the poetry written from April 1962, which includes 'Among the Narcissi', as "poems of an otherworldly, menacing landscape." Along with this new, fresh voice, the one we have come to see as Plath at the peak of her powers, there is a change in her use of nature imagery. It has now become a site of what Sally Bayley, in her essay on the sublime in Plath's tree poems, calls "subjective transference".

In *The Colossus*, Plath introduces us to her unique voice and multi-layered poems, which are often working at the symbolic, confessional, and psychological level simultaneously. Here, even in the seemingly simple countryside poems, Plath has created a natural world which is wrapped up and merged with other themes. In 'The Bull of Bendylaw', for example, the agricultural realm has merged with the mythic world of a kingdom by the sea, a genre blend that depicts the bull's conquest of the royal couple as a political coup. Similarly in 'Mushrooms' the political metaphor is invisible in the first two stanzas, but by the third stanza, the allegory emerges and the proliferation of fungus is both personal and a bid for power made by the collective. By the end of the poem, the collective will "inherit the earth."

'The Manor Garden', Plath's opening poem to her first-published collection, was written in the autumn of 1959 at the Yaddo Artist's Colony, a retreat set in 400 acres of woodland in upstate New York. The poem is about the baby she is expecting and it uses images from the natural world to create an atmosphere of dread: "the fountains are dry and the roses over". Fruit is depicted to point to fertility – the pears ripening – and its impending climax. Further into the poem, animals become symbols of a waiting dark inheritance. While the speaker wishes to bless the child, her biological anxieties overshadow her joy. Suicides are represented as wolves and a spider, worms and birds gather to usher in "a difficult borning." The moving, converging animals create an atmosphere of looming change, pointing to the poet's fear of losing her individual identity to motherhood when she still has so much artistic ambition (as explored in Clark's *Red Comet*.) The "difficult borning" operates both on the level of the child's birth and the poet's artistic birth.

In 'Faun', a faun who might really be a drunken man staggering home is watched by a group of owls perched on a tree. The poem has a haunting quality to it, and the metamorphosis of faun into man and back into faun under the gaze of the nocturnal bird enhances the sense of uncanny. Here, Plath creates a gothic vignette inside fifteen lines that highlights the mysteries of nature. The circularity of the faun-man-faun narrative also lends a surreal quality to the landscape of the piece. The image of birds perching on a tree is repeated deeper into the collection in 'Black Rook in Rainy Weather', where the speaker seeks conversation, if not communion, with the natural world: "I admit, I desire,/ Occasionally, some backtalk/ From the mute sky". The speaker is on a walk in the rain and is arrested by the vision of a rook rearranging its plume. The bird inspires a meditation on wonder with the spiritual language of angels, miracles and the celestial being used to dramatise the speaker's internal scepticism of religion. What the rook does provide is "respite from neutrality", that is, proof of relief against the blues, and by the end of the poem the bird has gone beyond representing wonder; it is the angel itself. Plath's merging of the natural and spiritual realms here evokes the American tradition of transcendentalism, where nature is a psycho-spiritual space.

Crossing the Water was published in 1971 and comprises of the poems written between *The Colossus* and *Ariel*. This collection is full of poetry that explores nature both as a theme and as a springboard for experimentation with voice, mood, and allegory. In this compilation of remainders, there are several poems that continue the trope of the speaker walking through a natural landscape that we see in 'Black Rook'. The walking poems 'Wuthering Heights', 'Parliament Hill Fields', 'Blackberrying' and 'Among the Narcissi' have the qualities of density and drama found in flash fiction and vividly show the psychic relationship between speaker and environment.

'Wuthering Heights' opens with the speaker walking towards the horizons and it is the horizons that hold power, using the active tense as they "ring", "warm", "singe" and "pin" all the while being "tilted" and "unstable." This surreal landscape, made more discomforting by being the location of the house on the moors that inspired Emily Bronte's novel, creates an almost mythic natural world that is simultaneously real (Plath walked these moors), literary, surreal in its painterly use of colour, and dangerously dynamic in how it can impact the speaker's psyche. In turn the speaker's mind – full of gloom and disturbia – colours what it sees; the sheep's coats are as "grey as the weather", and they almost morph into villains from a fairy tale, the phrase "grandmotherly disguise" summoning up images of a wolf in sheep's clothing and the grandmother-wolf in the Red Riding Hood story, so casting the speaker as almost childlike in her sense of fear.

In 'Parliament Hill Fields' the menacing surreal gives way to the surreal of grief, wherein the inner world is represented by the outer world. It is a poem about miscarriage and the natural world is used to show loss, incompleteness, and faded joy through such images as the "bald hill" and the "wan sun." The distortion of vision is both literal, as the speaker is seeing through tears, and psychological, hence the speaker sees gulls arguing and a line of little girls as a threatening crocodile. The lost child is the "ghost of a leaf, ghost of a bird". The conjuring of cypresses, the tree that symbolises mourning in Greek mythology, is compounded by the description that they are brooding and "dark-boughed", further intensified with the phrase "rooted in their heaped losses." When solace appears it is in the form of the older child, who is represented by a second hill, "the little pale blue hill" which "starts to glow" in her nursery. Here Plath shows that even an image of nature has the figurative power to heal, building on its capacity for relief and respite as shown in 'Black Rook'.

Nature as healer is explored more deeply in the closing poem of *Crossing the Water*. In 'Among the Narcissi' the speaker tells the story of Percy, an elderly man "recuperating from something on the lung," by walking through the spring fields of narcissi flowers. The striking image of the old man bowing references both his stooping back and the field of flowers made to bow by the wind. This mimesis between human and flower also highlights another exchange – that between sick person and healer. Percy "nurses his stitches" in this field, like a child getting its nutrients. In the third stanza there is a majesty attributed to Percy's bowing and persistent walking. Even while he is being mended by "flowers vivid as bandages", they are also suffering, connecting humans and nature through the shared experience of a life cycle.

Plath's hospital poem 'Tulips' portrays a period of time when the poet received a bouquet of tulips while recovering from an appendectomy. In contrast to the healing powers of Percy's narcissi, the flowers in 'Tulips' are harmful, "too red in the first place". The speaker imagines that the "redness talks to my wounds", and that the tulips watch her and "eat my oxygen". The arrival of the bouquet has inspired a paranoia in the speaker, taking on her medical anxiety, taking up her air and in a most striking image, they are as dangerous as an apex predator: "opening like the mouth of some great African cat." The speaker resents the way the tulips both distract and focus her at the same time, pointing to an indecisive split self.

In *Ariel: The Restored Edition,* the stark change in style from *The Colossus* manifests in the nature poems by further intensifying what Bayley calls the "sublime's aesthetic extremities", so that nature becomes a location for further experimentation with psychological landscapes. In her essay on Plath's tree poems, she singles out 'Elm' and traces its many drafts to show how Plath uses the figure of the elm tree as a location of subjective transference. An experimental leap has taken place since the transitional poems of *Crossing the Water,* and instead of being a botanical sketch or merely a symbol in 'Elm', the eponymous tree embodies the speaker's "I". The tree tells its story, but: "instead of holding together two distinct worlds of speaker and Nature the poem metonymically merges the natural canvas of the speaker's body, the figure of the "white" Godiva, into Nature's own canvas" (Bayley). This brings in an autobiographical reading, where Plath's own search for identity and self-creation is expressed through the desire to put down roots; "I know the bottom." Trees in Plath's world visually call upon the nervous system and symbolise personal growth and self-discovery. In 'Elm', the personification of the tree leads to both expansion and fragmentation. The tree houses more "I"s (the bird that lives in it) but also undergoes an identity crisis because it has suffered.

This identity crisis is dramatised further in 'The Moon and the Yew Tree' where the ominous landscape is a location for both self-construction and fragmentation. This push and pull relationship between the speaker, the moon and the tree creates an anxiety around wholeness while the speaker seeks "new forms of consciousness" (Bayley). Can the tree contain the light of the moon, which is the light of the mind? Can the tree carry the burden of the moon's despair? This poem problematises that which has been taken for granted so far, that the natural world is a foundation, a resting point and is always there to be personified and worn. In fusing the psychological and natural landscapes, Plath creates a world in which fragmentation of the "I" that has lost its way ("I simply cannot see where there is to get to") must take place, leading to a land of "blackness and silence."

In the collection's title poem, 'Ariel', this blackness and silence opens the poem ("stasis in darkness") and becomes an oblivion that is optimistically represented as a kind of freedom. We cut to meet the speaker in the midst of the gallop as the blur of blue conveys the speed of the horse she rides. Ariel herself is so powerful she is a creature from divine realms – God's lioness rather than a horse – who "hauls me through air–". Whilst in 'The Moon and the Yew Tree', the speaker ensures to note that the moon is not a door, in 'Ariel', the animal is a vehicle of transportation both in the story and metaphorically. The horse and its quality of speed turns the speaker into an arrow, an arrow with a specific mark: "the cauldron of morning." This final image invokes both the gothic and the spiritual, with the morning representing rebirth.

Across Plath's body of work, nature marks the passing of time. It signals change, often being used as subject material for symbolic development. Wrapped up in the abundance of nature imagery are other stories – of the Romantic sublime imagination through the lens of a 1950s context, the confessional narratives that have led to the poet's mythologisation, a rich and complex exploration of the poetic speaker's voice and the way in which it brings together the natural, psychological and surreal realms; the speaker's desire to be lost in and through nature as vehicle. Ultimately, Plath's personal ecopoetics, that is the way in which her poetic voice related to its created environment, become richer and more complex over the arc of her poetry collections, gifting us with a poetic universe that allows nature to be symbol, canvas, and portal to a new world.

Works Cited and Reference Texts:

The Colossus, Sylvia Plath, Faber, 2008 (first published 1960)

Crossing the Water, Sylvia Plath, Faber, 2017, (first published 1971)

Ariel, The Restored Edition, Sylvia Plath, Faber, 2004 (first published 1965)

Representing Sylvia Plath, edited by Sally Bayley and Tracy Brain, Cambridge University Press, 2011,

Chapter 5 " 'The trees of the mind are black, the light is blue' - sublime encounters in Sylvia Plath's tree poems", Sally Bayley.

"On Sylvia Plath's Creative Breakthrough at the Yaddo Artists' Colony", Heather Clark, https://lithub.com/on-sylvia-plaths-creative-breakthrough-at-the-yaddo-artists-colony/, 2020, Excerpted from *Red Comet: The Short Life and Blazing Art of Sylvia Plath* by Heather Clark.

FURTHER READING

Sylvia Plath bibliography (UK editions)

1960. *The Colossus*. Faber & Faber.

1963. *The Bell Jar*. Faber & Faber.

1965. *Ariel*. Faber & Faber.

1971. *Crossing the Water*. Faber & Faber.

1971. *Winter Trees*. Faber & Faber.

1975. Plath, Sylvia, and Aurelia Schober Plath. *Letters Home Correspondence, 1950-1963*. Faber & Faber.

1977. *Johnny Panic and the Bible of Dreams and Other Prose Writings*. Faber & Faber.

1981. Plath, Sylvia, and Ted Hughes. *Sylvia Plath Collected Poems*. Faber & Faber.

2000. Plath, Sylvia, and Karen V. Kukil. *The Journals of Sylvia Plath, 1950-1962*. Faber & Faber.

2001. Plath, Sylvia, and David Roberts. *Collected Children's Stories*. Faber & Faber.

2004. Plath, Sylvia, Frieda Hughes, and David Semanki. *Ariel the Restored Edition; A Facsimile of Plath's Manuscript Reinstating Her Original Selection and Arrangement*. Faber & Faber.

2017/2019. Plath, Sylvia, Peter K. Steinberg, and Karen V. Kukil. *The Letters of Sylvia Plath Volumes 1 and 2*. Faber & Faber.

WIDER READING

Tracy Brain, *The Other Sylvia Plath*, Taylor & Francis, 2001

Heather Clark, *Red Comet: The Short Life and Blazing Art of Sylvia Plath*, Vintage, 2022

Heather Clark,*The Grief of Influence: Sylvia Plath and Ted Hughes, OUP, 2010*

Gail Crowther, *Three Martini Afternoons at the Ritz: The Rebellion of Sylvia Plath and Anne Sexton*, Gallery, 2021

Gail Crowther,*The Haunted Reader*, Fonthill, 2017

Jo Gill, *The Cambridge Introduction to Sylvia Plath*, CUP 2008

Tim Kendall, *Sylvia Plath: A Critical Guide*, Faber and Faber 2001

Janet Malcom, *The Silent Woman: Sylvia Plath and Ted Hughes*, Granta, 2012

Jaqueline Rose, *The Haunting of Sylvia Plath*, Virago, 2013

ACKNOWLEDGEMENTS & THANKS

A huge thank you to each of our sixty contributors for their work, imagination and creativity. Sylvia Plath inspired you, and *After Sylvia* would not exist without you. Our gratitude to everyone who entered one (or more) of the three poetry competitions that provided over a dozen poems for the anthology: The Sylvia Plath Prize, The Young Poets Network's Sylvia Plath Challenge, and the Poetry Society's Members' Competition (summer 2022).

In 2021, the *After Sylvia* project was awarded an Arts Council National Lottery Project Grant. We extend our thanks to both Arts Council England and the National Lottery, and to Arts Council England's Stephen May for his much-valued support and encouragement. We are also very grateful to our official partners, the Poetry Society and the Manchester Poetry Library, for their guidance and practical help over the past eighteen months.

Epigraph from 'Morning Song' by Sylvia Plath (from *Sylvia Plath Collected Poems,* Faber & Faber, 1981) reproduced by permission of Faber & Faber.

Special thanks to Louise Crosby for designing the striking *After Sylvia* book cover. And thank you, of course, to the inimitable Jane Commane at Nine Arches Press. Many thanks also to Frieda Hughes for giving the *After Sylvia* project her blessing.

Finally, the biggest thank you of all to Sylvia Plath for providing the spark.

Project partners:

Supported using public funding by:

THEPOETRYSOCIETY

BIOGRAPHIES

Moniza Alvi was born in Lahore to an English mother and a Pakistani father. She grew up in Hertfordshire. Her first collection *The Country at My Shoulder* (Oxford University Press, 1993) was shortlisted for the T. S. Eliot and the Whitbread poetry prizes and selected for the New Generation Poets promotion. *Europa* (Bloodaxe, 2008) and *At the Time of Partition* (Bloodaxe, 2013) were both Poetry Book Society Choices and shortlisted for the T. S. Eliot Prize. She has a new collection *Fairoz* (Bloodaxe, 2022).

Romalyn Ante is a Filipino-British, Wolverhampton-based author. She is co-founding editor of *harana poetry,* a magazine for poets who write in English as a second or parallel language, and founder of *Tsaá with Roma,* an online interview series with poets and other artists. Her debut collection is *Antiemetic for Homesickness* (Chatto & Windus). She was recently awarded the Jerwood Compton Poetry Fellowship 2021/22.

Mona Arshi's debut collection *Small Hands* (Pavilion Poetry, 2015) won the Forward Prize for Best First Collection in 2015. Her second collection *Dear Big Gods* was published in April 2019. Her poems and interviews have been published in *The Times, Guardian, Granta* and *The Times of India* as well as on the London Underground. During 2021 Mona was poet in residence in a bird sanctuary in Cley Marshes, Norfolk. Her debut novel, *Somebody Loves You,* was published in 2021 by And Other Stories. It was longlisted for the 2022 Jhalak Prize and the 2022 Desmond Elliott Prize.

Polly Atkin is a poet and nonfiction writer, living in the English Lake District. Her first poetry collection *Basic Nest Architecture* (Seren: 2017) is followed by *Much With Body* (Seren, 2021). Her biography *Recovering Dorothy: The Hidden Life of Dorothy Wordsworth* (Saraband, 2021), is the first to focus on Dorothy's later life and illness. Her next book is a memoir in essays exploring place, belonging and disability. In 2022 she became a Fellow of the Royal Society of Literature.

Tiffany Atkinson's most recent collection is *Lumen,* a Poetry Book Society Recommendation and winner of the Medicine Unboxed Creative Prize, published by Bloodaxe in 2021. She lives in Norwich and is professor of poetry at the University of East Anglia where she convenes the MA in Creative Writing (Poetry). She is currently finishing a book of criticism about poetry, ethics and embarrassment.

Sally Baker works for The Reader organisation and teaches poetry in adult education. She likes growing flowers, especially tulips, and collects ships in bottles. Her poems have appeared in various poetry magazines and anthologies, and a pamphlet *The Sea and The Forest* was published by The Poetry Business a long time ago. One day she might have enough poems for a collection. She is currently studying for a PhD in Place Writing Studies at Manchester Metropolitan University.

Colin Bancroft is currently working on a PhD on the Ecopoetics of Robert Frost. His pamphlet *Impermanence* was released with Maytree Press in 2020 and *Kayfabe* with Broken Sleep | Legitimate Snack in 2021. His pamphlet *Knife Edge* was released in April 2022 with Broken Sleep. He won the Poets and Players Prize in 2016, and was joint winner of the Picador Shore to Shore and Manchester Cathedral Poetry Competitions (2021) respectively. He is editor at Nine Pens Press.

Emily Berry is the author of three poetry books: *Dear Boy* (2013), *Stranger, Baby* (2017) and *Unexhausted Time* (2022). Her lyric essay on agoraphobia, dreams and the imagination, 'The Secret Country of Her Mind', appears in the artist's book *Many Nights* (2021) by Jacqui Kenny. She is a fellow of the Royal Society of Literature and lives in London, where she was born.

Nina Billard Sarmadi: I first started writing poetry at the age of nine. London inspires me as no other city does: its wildlife, cityscapes and myriad cultures just write themselves in my head. On a Sunday morning, I tend to be sipping a mug of hot chocolate, along with a dog-eared book and a croissant. Either a large book of botany or an excellent murder mystery will do – well, that is to say, that – and everything else in-between!

Caroline Bird is a poet and playwright. Her 2020 collection, *The Air Year*, won the Forward Prize for Best Collection 2020 and was shortlisted for the Polari Prize and the Costa Prize. Her fifth collection, *In These Days of Prohibition*, was shortlisted for the 2017 T. S. Eliot Prize and the Ted Hughes Award. She won an Eric Gregory Award in 2002 and was shortlisted for the Geoffrey Dearmer Prize in 2001 and the Dylan Thomas Prize in 2008 and 2010. She was one of the five official poets at the 2012 London Olympics. As a playwright, Bird has been shortlisted for the George Devine Award and the Susan Smith Blackburn Prize. Her Selected Poems, *Rookie*, was published in May 2022.

Sharon Black is from Glasgow and lives in a remote valley of the Cévennes mountains. Her poetry is published widely and prizes include the Guernsey International Poetry Prize 2019 and *The London*

Magazine Poetry Prizes 2019 and 2018. Her collections are *To Know Bedrock* (Pindrop, 2011), *The Art of Egg* (Two Ravens, 2015; Pindrop, 2019) and a pamphlet, *Rib* (Wayleave, 2021). Her third and fourth full collections will appear in 2022 with Vagabond Voices and with Drunk Muse Press respectively. www.sharonblack.co.uk

David Borrott lives in Lancashire with his partner and their three sons. He has a cherry tree in his front garden and a yew tree in the back. His pamphlet *Porthole* was published by Smith/ Doorstop.

Mary Jean Chan is the author of *Flèche*, published by Faber & Faber (2019) and Faber USA (2020). *Flèche* won the 2019 Costa Book Award for Poetry and was shortlisted in 2020 for the International Dylan Thomas Prize, John Pollard Foundation International Poetry Prize, Jhalak Prize and Seamus Heaney Centre First Collection Poetry Prize. In 2021, *Flèche* was a Lambda Literary Award Finalist. Chan won the 2018 Geoffrey Dearmer Prize and was shortlisted for the Forward Prize for Best Single Poem in 2017 and 2019, receiving an Eric Gregory Award in 2019. Chan is a Senior Lecturer in Creative Writing (Poetry) at Oxford Brookes University and lives in Oxford.

Heather Clark is Professor of Contemporary Poetry at the University of Huddersfield, and the author of *The Ulster Renaissance: Poetry in Belfast 1962-1972* (Oxford UP); *The Grief of Influence: Sylvia Plath and Ted Hughes* (Oxford UP); and *Red Comet: The Short Life and Blazing Art of Sylvia Plath* (Knopf/Jonathan Cape), which was a finalist for the Pulitzer Prize, the National Book Critics Circle Award, and the LA Times Book Prize, and won the Slightly Foxed Prize for Best First Biography. She is currently working on a new book about the Boston years of Sylvia Plath, Anne Sexton, Adrienne Rich, and Maxine Kumin.

Angela Cleland is a Scottish poet and novelist. Cleland has worked as a supermarket store detective, a knowledge engineer, a business analyst and as the development manager for an award-winning e-learning company. She now lives in Surrey with her husband and two sons, where she works as a poetry tutor and audio-narrator. She is the author of two collections of poetry, *And in Here the Menagerie* (Templar Poetry) and *Room of Thieves* (Salt Publishing), and one novel, *Sequela* (as Cleland Smith). Her third collection, *Real Cute Danger*, will be published by Broken Sleep Books in December 2022. @AngelaCleland www.angelacleland.co.uk

Jane Commane is director/editor at Nine Arches Press, co-editor of Under the Radar magazine and co-author (with Jo Bell) of *How to Be a Poet*. Her debut poetry collection, *Assembly Lines* (Bloodaxe, 2018) was longlisted for the 2019 Michael Murphy Memorial Prize. Her poetry has featured in Staying Human (Bloodaxe) and in *The Guardian, Butcher's Dog* and *Poetry Birmingham Literary Journal*. She is a Writing West Midlands' Room 204 writer, and in 2017 was awarded a Jerwood Compton Poetry Fellowship.

Sarah Corbett has published five collections of poetry, including the verse-novel, *And She Was* (Pavilion Poetry, 2015), and most recently *A Perfect Mirror* (Pavilion Poetry, 2018). Her first collection, *The Red Wardrobe* (Seren books, 1998) won an Eric Gregory Award and was shortlisted for the Forward Best First Collection Prize and the T. S. Eliot Prize. She also writes fiction, and has won two Northern Writers Awards for fiction. A new poetry book is forthcoming from Pavilion in 2024. Sarah is Senior Lecturer in Creative Writing for Lancaster University and lives in Hebden Bridge. She is Director of the Sylvia Plath Literary Festival, 2022.

Jonah Corren Hailing from West Dorset, Jonah Corren is a songwriter-poet. His work has been anthologised by Nine Pens Press, Acid Bath Publishing and Bad Betty Press, and published online by Young Poets' Network, *Violet Indigo Blue, etc*, and others. He is a UniSlam champion (2019), and an alumnus of BBC New Creatives (2019/20) and The Apples & Snakes Writing Room (2021). His debut alt-folk EP, *Dreaming and Petty Crime,* was released in December 2020.

Dr Gail Crowther is a freelance writer, researcher, and academic who specialises in Sylvia Plath studies, Anne Sexton, archives, place, and sociological hauntings. Her latest book, *Three-Martini Afternoons at The Ritz,* is a dual biography exploring the social rebellion of Sylvia Plath and Anne Sexton. This was published by Simon & Schuster, New York, in April 2021. She is currently working on her second book for Simon & Schuster.

Mari Ellis Dunning's poems and short fiction can be found in recent editions of *Poetry Wales, New Welsh Reader* and *The Ghastling*, amongst others. She is author of *Salacia* (Parthian), which was shortlisted for the Wales Book of the Year Award in 2019, *Pearl & Bone* (Parthian) and co-author of *The Wrong Side of the Looking Glass* (Black Rabbit Press). Mari is a PhD candidate at Aberystwyth University, where she is writing a historic novel exploring the relationship between accusations of witchcraft and the female body. She lives on the west coast of Wales, in Llanon, with her husband, their two sons and their dog.

Samatar Elmi: winner of the 2021 Geoffrey Dearmer Prize, Samatar is an Obsidian Fellow, Numbi Associate Poetry Editor and graduate of the Young Inscribe Mentoring Program. Poems have appeared in *Poetry Review, Magma, Iota* and anthologised in *More Fiya, Filigree* and *The Echoing Gallery.* Elmi's *Portrait of Colossus* was selected for the PBS Summer Pamphlet Choice. As Knomad Spock, his most recent album, *Winter of Discontent* was critically acclaimed in print (*Clash Magazine, Afropunk, GoldFlakePaint, Equate Magazine*) and radio (BBC 6 Music, BBC Wales, Amazing Radio, Radio X).

Ruth Fainlight has published 17 collections of poems since 1966. Her *New & Collected Poems* was published in 2010, and her most recent collection, *Somewhere Else Entirely,* in 2018.

Daniel Fraser is a writer from Hebden Bridge, Yorkshire. His poetry and prose have won prizes and been published widely in print and online, including: *London Magazine, Magma, LA Review of Books*, *Aeon*, *Hobart, Poetry Birmingham, Radical Philosophy* and *Review 31.* His debut poetry pamphlet *Lung Iron* is published by **ignition**press. A current Humanities Excellence Scholar at University College Cork, his research examines trauma and temporality in post-WWII European literature.

Rosie Garland writes long and short fiction, poetry and sings with post-punk band The March Violets. Her work appears in *The Guardian, Spelk, Interpreter's House, The Rialto, Ellipsis, Butcher's Dog, Mslexia, The North* and elsewhere. Latest poetry collection *What Girls do in the Dark* (Nine Arches Press) was shortlisted for The Polari Prize 2021. Val McDermid has named her one of the UK's most compelling LGBT+ writers. She has a passion for language nurtured by public libraries, and a firm belief in the power of persistence. www.rosiegarland.com

Victoria Gatehouse lives in West Yorkshire and combines writing with a day job in medical research. Her work has been widely published in magazines and anthologies and also broadcast on BBC Radio. Competition wins include The Ilkley Festival Poetry Prize, the PENfro Poetry Prize, The Poetry News Members' Competition and the Indigo International Wild Nature Poetry Award. Victoria's second pamphlet,

The Mechanics of Love, published by smith I doorstop, was selected as a 'Laureate's Choice' by Carol Ann Duffy in 2019.

Rebecca Goss is a poet and mentor living in Suffolk. She is the author of three full-length collections and two pamphlets. Her second collection, *Her Birth,* (Carcanet/Northern House 2013) was shortlisted for the 2013 Forward Prize for Best Collection, won the Poetry category in the East Anglian Book Awards 2013, and in 2015 was shortlisted for the Warwick Prize for Writing and the Portico Prize for Literature. In 2014 she was selected for the Poetry Book Society's Next Generation Poets. She has an MA in Creative Writing from Cardiff University and a PhD by Publication from the University of East Anglia.

Annie Hayter is a writer from South London who delights in the foibles of queer mythmaking. They won BBC Proms Young Poet, were shortlisted for The White Review's Poet's Prize, Young People's Laureate for London & came 3rd in Cúirt New Writing Prize for Poetry. They have words in: *The Big Issue, Token Magazine, Tentacular, MAGMA, Time Out, The Log Books Podcast,* & *Bedtime Stories for the End of the World Podcast.*

Gaia Holmes is a poet, writing tutor and pet/house sitter. She lives in Halifax in a tiny flat above the tree line on the top floor of a ramshackle Georgian mansion. She is currently working on her debut collection of short stories.

Ian Humphreys lives in West Yorkshire. His debut collection *Zebra* (Nine Arches Press, 2019) was nominated for the Portico Prize. He is the editor of *Why I Write Poetry* (Nine Arches Press, 2021), and the producer and co-editor of *After Sylvia* (Nine Arches Press, 2022). Ian's work has been highly commended in the Forward Prizes for Poetry and won first prize in the Hamish Canham Prize. His poems are widely published in journals, including *The Poetry Review* and *Poetry London,* and he has written for the BBC. Ian is a fellow of The Complete Works.

Julie Irigaray's debut pamphlet *Whalers, Witches and Gauchos* was published by Nine Pens in 2021. Her poems appeared internationally (US, UK, Ireland, Italy, Mexico, Canada, Singapore and South Korea) in *The Rialto, Ambit; Magma;* and *Stand.* She was commended in the 2020 Ambit Magazine Poetry Prize and selected as one of the 50 Best New British and Irish Poets 2018 (Eyewear Publishing), among other prizes. She is doing a PhD on Sylvia Plath, England and her transnational identity at the University of Huddersfield.

Bhanu Kapil is a poet, and Fellow of Churchill College. *How To Wash A Heart*, her most recent collection, won the T. S. Eliot Prize and was a Poetry Book Society Choice.

Victoria Kennefick's debut poetry collection, *Eat or We Both Starve* (Carcanet, 2021), won the Seamus Heaney First Collection Poetry Prize 2022 and the Dalkey Book Festival Emerging Writer of the Year Award 2022. It has been shortlisted for the Derek Walcott Prize for Poetry 2022 and in 2021 was shortlisted for both the T.S. Eliot Prize and the Costa Poetry Book Award. Victoria is the current poet in residence at the Yeats Society Sligo.

Martin Kratz's reviews and translations from the German have appeared in *MPT* and *Agenda*. Recent translations were anthologised in *The Heart of a Stranger: An Anthology of Exile Literature* (Pushkin Press, 2019). He is the co-editor of *Mount London: Ascents in the Vertical City* (Penned in the Margins, 2014). His pamphlet, *A Skeleton's Progress* (Poetry Salzburg), was published in 2018. He is Programme Manager at Manchester Poetry Library.

Zaffar Kunial was born in Birmingham and lives in Hebden Bridge. He is a recipient of Yale University's Windham-Campbell Prize and his first poetry collection, *Us*, published by Faber & Faber in 2018 appeared on a number of shortlists including the Costa Poetry Award and the T. S. Eliot Prize. 'Tulips' is published in his second collection, *England's Green*, which is a PBS Autumn 2022 recommendation.

Jennifer Lee Tsai is a poet and critic. She was born in Bebington and grew up in Liverpool. Jennifer is a fellow of The Complete Works programme for diversity and innovation and a Ledbury Poetry Critic. Her work is widely published in magazines and journals as well as in the Bloodaxe anthology *Ten: Poets of the New Generation* (2017). Jennifer's debut poetry pamphlet is *Kismet* (**ignition**press, 2019). In 2019, she was awarded an AHRC scholarship to undertake doctoral research in Creative Writing at the University of Liverpool. She is the winner of a Northern Writers Award for Poetry 2020. Her second poetry pamphlet is forthcoming in Autumn 2022.

Carola Luther's most recent collection *On the Way to Jerusalem Farm* was published by Carcanet Press in September 2021, and has been shortlisted for the Derek Walcott Prize for Poetry (2022). Her two earlier collections, *Walking the Animals* (2004) and *Arguing with Malarchy* (2011) were also published by Carcanet Press.

Karen McCarthy Woolf: Born in London to English and Jamaican parents, Karen McCarthy Woolf's first poetry collection *An Aviary of Small Birds* was nominated for the Forward Felix Dennis and Jerwood Prizes and her latest *Seasonal Disturbances* was a winner in the inaugural Laurel Prize.

Roy McFarlane is a Poet, Playwright and former Youth & Community Worker born in Birmingham of Jamaican parentage, living in Brighton. He's the National Canal Laureate and was a former Birmingham Poet Laureate. His debut collection, *Beginning With Your Last Breath*, was followed by *The Healing Next Time,* (Nine Arches Press 2018) nominated for the Ted Hughes award and Jhalak Prize. His third collection *Living by Troubled Waters* coming out October 2022. Roy loves Jazz and walking with herons.

Nina Mingya Powles is a writer, poet, zinemaker and librarian from Aotearoa, New Zealand, currently living in London. Her debut poetry collection *Magnolia* 木蘭 was shortlisted for the 2020 Forward Prize for Best First Book of Poetry. Her food memoir, *Tiny Moons*, was published by The Emma Press in 2020. In 2019 she won the Nan Shepherd Prize for Nature Writing; her resulting collection of essays *Small Bodies of Water* was published in 2021.

Mark Pajak was born in Merseyside. He has written for The BBC, *The Guardian, The London Review of Books, Poetry London, The North, The Rialto* and Magma. He has been three times included in the National Poetry Competition winners list, awarded first place in The Bridport Prize and has also received a Northern Writers' Award, an Eric Gregory Award and an UNESCO international writing residency. His first pamphlet, *Spitting Distance,* was selected by Carol Ann Duffy as a Laureate's Choice and is published with smith|doorstop. His first full-length collection, *Slide*, is published with Cape.

Caleb Parkin, Bristol City Poet 2020 - 22, has poems in *The Guardian, The Rialto, The Poetry Review, Under the Radar, Poetry Wales, Magma, Butcher's Dog* and elsewhere. He won second prize in the National Poetry Competition 2016, Winchester Poetry Prize 2017 and other shortlists. He tutors for Poetry Society, Poetry School, Cheltenham Festivals, First Story, Arvon and holds an MSc in Creative Writing for Therapeutic Purposes. Debut pamphlet, *Wasted Rainbow* (tall-lighthouse). Debut collection *This Fruiting Body* (Nine Arches Press). In 2022, he'll publish a new pamphlet with Broken Sleep and his collected City Poet work.

Pascale Petit was born in Paris and lives in Cornwall. She is of French, Welsh, and Indian heritage. Her eighth collection, *Tiger Girl* (Bloodaxe Books, 2020), was shortlisted for the Forward Prize and for Wales Book of the Year. A poem from the book won the Keats-Shelley Prize. Her seventh collection, *Mama Amazonica* (Bloodaxe Books, 2017), won the inaugural Laurel Prize for eco-poetry, and the RSL's Ondaatje Prize. Four previous collections were shortlisted for the T. S. Eliot Prize. Petit is widely translated and travelled, particularly in the Amazon rainforest and India.

Jacob Polley won the 2016 T. S. Eliot Prize for poetry for his fourth book of poems, *Jackself*. He is Professor of Creative Writing at Newcastle University and lives with his family on the north east coast.

Niamh Prior lives in County Cork, Ireland, not far from where she grew up by the Atlantic Ocean. She studied English with Film and TV Studies at Brunel University London, and later Creative Writing at UCC, where her postgraduate work was funded by the Irish Research Council. Her poetry and short stories have appeared in publications including *The North*, *Southword* and *The Stinging Fly*. She is the author of a novel, *Catchlights*, published by John Murray Originals.

Shivanee Ramlochan is an Indo-Caribbean poet and the author of *Unkillable* (Noemi Press, 2022) and *Everyone Knows I Am a Haunting* (Peepal Tree Press, 2017). The recipient of residencies and grants from Catapult Caribbean Arts, Bread Loaf, and Millay Arts, she lives in Las Lomas, Trinidad.

Clara Rosarius is a native of Cologne, Germany, but grew up in New York City. She is currently an undergraduate at Oberlin College. In 2018, she attended the Iowa Young Writers' Workshop, where she studied poetry. She has received a National Silver Medal for poetry from the Scholastic Art & Writing Awards and the Principles Award for Creativity from Elisabeth Irwin High School. She was a finalist for the 2021 Adroit Prize for Prose.

Devina Shah is a writer and critic based in London. She studied English and Modern Languages (French) at Wadham College, Oxford. She is the founder and editor of *Quince Magazine,* (www.quincemag.com) an online literary and visual arts journal featuring work by writers and artists from around the world. Recently she has reviewed collections for The Poetry School (Bhanu Kapil's *How to Wash a Heart*) and *Modern Poetry in Translation* (Anna Greki's *Streets of Algiers* and Ribka Sibhatu's *Aulò! Aulò! Aulò!*). Devina is a 2021 Ledbury Critic.

Penelope Shuttle lives in Cornwall. Her thirteenth collection, *Lyonesse,* appeared from Bloodaxe in June 2021, and was *Observer* Poetry Book of the Month for July. *Covid/Corvid,* a pamphlet written in collaboration with Alyson Hallett, was published by Broken Sleep Books, September 2021. *Father Lear,* a pamphlet, was published by Poetry Salzburg, 2020.

Jean Sprackland has published five poetry collections, most recently *Green Noise* (Cape, 2018). Her book *Tilt* won the Costa Poetry Award in 2007. She is also the author of two books of prose non-fiction, *Strands* and *These Silent Mansions.* Jean is Professor of Creative Writing at Manchester Metropolitan University.

Laura Stanley is a lesbian poet from the West Midlands. Her heresy has been published in *Magma, bath magg* and *streetcake*. In 2020, she won the Staunch Short Story Prize. In 2021, she won third place in the Young Poet Network's Pop Culture Challenge.

Paul Stephenson studied modern languages and linguistics. He has published three pamphlets: *Those People* (Smith|Doorstop, 2015), which won the Poetry Business pamphlet competition; *The Days that Followed Paris* (Happen*Stance*, 2016), written while living in Paris at the time of the November 2015 terrorist attacks; and *Selfie with Waterlilies* (Paper Swans Press, 2017). In 2013/14 he took part in the Jerwood/Arvon mentoring scheme and the Aldeburgh Eight, before completing an MA in Creative Writing (Poetry) with the Manchester Writing School. In 2018 he co-edited the 'Europe' issue of *Magma* (70) and currently co-curates Poetry in Aldeburgh. He lives between Cambridge and Brussels.

Degna Stone is a cofounder of *Butcher's Dog* poetry magazine and a contributing editor at *The Rialto.* They are a recipient of a Northern Writers Award for poetry and their debut full length collection *Proof of Life on Earth* is forthcoming from Nine Arches Press.

Dorka Tamás has completed her PhD research at the University of Exeter. Her thesis explores the supernatural in Sylvia Plath's poetry by employing the theoretical framework of the early modern witch-hunt. Her research interest includes literary representations of magic and witchcraft and the relationship between the natural environment and supernatural subthemes across literature and culture, particularly in the works of Sylvia Plath. Dorka is also the co-founder of the Sylvia Plath Society. Her research has been published in *Feminist Modernist Studies, Plath Profiles*, and *USSO*. She is currently working on the essay

'Sylvia Plath behind the Iron Curtain' and turning her thesis into a monograph.

Anastasia Taylor-Lind is an English/Swedish photojournalist covering issues relating to women, war and violence. She is a *National Geographic Magazine* photographer, a TED fellow and a 2016 Harvard Nieman fellow. She writes poems about contemporary conflicts and the experiences she cannot photograph.

Peter Wallis is a Hawthornden Fellow, and Submissions Editor for the U.K. charity Poems in the Waiting Room. He won publication of a pamphlet, *Articles of Twinship*, in the *Bare Fiction* Debut Poetry Collection Competition 2015.

Tom Weir's poetry has been Highly Commended in both The Forward Prize and The National Poetry Competition. He has won the *Magma* Editor's Choice Prize and was one of the inaugural winners of the Templar IOTA Shots competition. He has published two full collections *All That Falling* and *Ruin*, for which he is grateful to have received a grant from the Arts Council. Having spent many years living in the north of England, he now lives in Bristol where he is working on his third collection.

Sarah Westcott grew up in north Devon and lives on the edge of London. Her first pamphlet, *Inklings*, was a Poetry Book Society pamphlet choice and *Slant Light* (Pavilion Poetry, 2016), was highly commended in the Forward Prize. Her second collection, *Bloom*, also with Pavilion Poetry, was published in 2021 and longlisted for The Laurel Prize 2022. Sarah was a news journalist for twenty years and now works as a freelance tutor, editor and writer. Work has appeared on beermats, billboards and buses, baked into sourdough bread and installed in a nature reserve, triggered by footsteps.

Merrie Joy Williams is a poet, novelist, writing tutor and editor. She was a winner of The Poetry Archive's 'Wordview 2020' competition, and has been longlisted twice for the National Poetry Competition, and shortlisted three times for The Bridport Prize. She is the recipient of London Writers' and Arts Council England awards, and has had residencies including Manchester Poetry Library and Historic England. Poems have appeared in *Poetry Wales, Pree Lit, The Good Journal, Tentacular, The Interpreter's House*, and elsewhere. Her debut collection is *Open Windows* (Waterloo Press, 2019).

Sarah Wimbush is a Yorkshire poet and a grateful recipient of a Northern Writers' Award. She recently released her first collection, *Shelling Peas with My Grandmother in the Gorgiolands* (Bloodaxe, 2022), having previously published two prize-winning pamphlets: *The Last Dinosaur in Doncaster* (Smith|Doorstop, 2021) and *Bloodlines* (Seren, 2020). Her poems have appeared in *Atrium, The Friday Poem, Lighthouse, Magma, Mslexia, The North, Poetry News, Poetry Wales, Stand* and *Butcher's Dog*, among others. Her Little Red poetry-film is available on YouTube: https://www.youtube.com/watch?v=C1vZf3MuwAg.

Tamar Yoseloff's sixth collection is *The Black Place* (Seren, 2019). She is also the author of *Formerly* (the inaugural chapbook from her publishing venture, Hercules Editions), incorporating photographs by Vici MacDonald and shortlisted for the 2012 Ted Hughes Award, and collaborative editions with the artists Linda Karshan and Charlotte Harker respectively. She has run courses for galleries including the Hayward, the RA and the National Gallery and co-curated the exhibition *A Fine Day for Seeing* at Southwark Park Galleries in 2021. She's a lecturer on the Poetry School / Newcastle University MA in Writing Poetry.